YORK NOTES

The Wife of Bath's Prologue and Tale

Geoffrey Chaucer

Notes by J. A. Tasioulas

 Longman   ⊕ York Press

YORK PRESS
322 Old Brompton Road, London SW5 9JH

Pearson Education Limited
Edinburgh Gate, Harlow,
Essex CM20 2JE, United Kingdom
Associated companies, branches and representatives throughout the world

First published 1998
Eighth impression 2007

ISBN 978-0-582-32926-3

Designed by Vicki Pacey, Trojan Horse, London
Phototypeset by Gem Graphics, Trenance, Mawgan Porth, Cornwall
Colour reproduction and film output by Spectrum Colour
Produced by Pearson Education Asia Limited, Hong Kong

CONTENTS

PART ONE

INTRODUCTION

HOW TO STUDY A NARRATIVE POEM

Studying a narrative poem on your own requires self-discipline and a carefully thought-out work plan in order to be effective.

- You will need to read the poem more than once. Start by reading it quickly for pleasure, then read it slowly and thoroughly.
- Look up all the words which you do not know. Some may have more than one meaning so note them. They may be intended to be ambiguous.
- On your second reading make detailed notes on the plot, characters and themes of the poem. Further readings will generate new ideas and help you to memorise the details.
- Think about how the poem is narrated. From whose point of view are the events described? Does your response to the narrator change at all in the course of the poem?
- The main character is the narrator, but what about the others? Do they develop? Do you only ever see them from the narrator's point of view?
- Identify what styles of language are used in the poem.
- Assess what the main arguments are in the poem. Who are the narrator's main opponents? Are their views ever fairly presented?
- Are words, images or incidents repeated so as to give the work a pattern? Do such patterns help you to understand the poem's themes?
- What is the effect of the poem's ending? Is the action completed and closed, or left incomplete and open?
- Does the poem present a world or point of view of which you are meant to approve?
- Cite exact sources for all quotations, whether from the text itself or from critical commentaries. Wherever possible find your own examples from the poem to back up your opinions.
- Always express your ideas in your own words.

This York Note offers an introduction to *The Wife of Bath's Prologue and Tale* and cannot substitute for close reading of the text and the study of secondary sources.

Chaucer's Wife of Bath, a middle-aged woman from the West Country, strides into *The Canterbury Tales* on a large horse, spurs jangling, and ready to assert herself in a company made up almost entirely of men. It is an extraordinary thing. Women in medieval literature do not tend to have the starring role. They feature in stories as beautiful ladies (usually in distress) or perhaps as old crones out to cause trouble. But the Wife of Bath is not a helpless noble lady nor can she be dismissed as a crone. There has in fact been nothing like her in English literature before. She is a medieval housewife who is not just going to star in a story, she is going to tell it.

The Wife of Bath's Prologue is the life story of Alison, five times married and eager to make it six. It is very unusual for an 'ordinary' woman to be the object of such literary interest. Chaucer certainly does not tell us so much about the other pilgrims in *The Canterbury Tales*. So what was he doing with the Wife of Bath? While there is very little medieval literature about medieval housewives, there is a lot of literature written which condemns women – all women, from the highest to the lowest. Chaucer does not ignore this. Instead, he uses it to form the Wife's character. He makes her large, noisy and bossy. She torments her husbands and has a great sexual appetite. But, on the other hand, she is capable of love, can be vulnerable and has great vitality and optimism. She also manages to argue against many of the medieval anti-women ideas. And so we are in a quandary. Are we supposed to sympathise with the Wife and view her as the first true defender of women's rights? Or is she an elaborate joke which makes women look even worse because the whole story is being told by a woman? Chaucer does not make it easy for us to decide. Our expectations are turned on their heads as we work through many layers of argument and attempt to unravel many ambiguities.

And if the *Wife of Bath's Prologue* is different from anything we have ever encountered before, so is *The Wife of Bath's Tale*. Nothing is what it seems. Our handsome knight is a rapist, our heroine is an ugly old woman and the damsel in distress is replaced by a court full of powerful women. All the traditional ideas about medieval women are brought sharply into focus in the course of *The Wife of Bath's Prologue and Tale*. But it is a matter for debate whether they are destroyed or strengthened in the course of the Wife's comic antics.

Part two

Summaries

The Wife of Bath's Prologue and Tale *is one of the twenty-four stories which make up* The Canterbury Tales. *This work was left unfinished by Chaucer when he died and the order in which he intended the tales to be read is not clear. The text makes it plain that the Wife of Bath should be followed by the Friar and then the Summoner but there is no indication of who should come before the Wife. Chaucer wrote before the invention of printing and his work therefore survives in manuscripts which would have been copied out by hand.*

The standard edition of the complete works of Chaucer is Larry D. Benson, ed., The Riverside Chaucer, *Houghton Mifflin, 1987. A single edition of the text can be found in James Winny, ed.,* The Wife of Bath's Prologue and Tale, *Cambridge University Press, 1965, on which these Notes are based.*

Synopsis

The Wife of Bath first appears in the *General Prologue*, right at the beginning of *The Canterbury Tales*. She is a slightly deaf, gap-toothed, mature woman with a ruddy complexion and a flamboyant taste in clothes. She earns her living in the cloth trade but most of her portrait focuses on her personal life and we are told that she has had five husbands. Thus, in the *General Prologue*, where each of the characters is described in terms of his or her profession, the Wife of Bath is clearly a 'professional wife'. She is also very nearly a professional pilgrim, having travelled further than almost all the other pilgrims. What we are presented with here, therefore, is a larger than life character, bold, adventurous and sociable, but also one who will not tolerate being placed in an inferior position.

The Wife of Bath's Prologue begins with the Wife bursting onto the scene, and declaring that she will speak of the woe that is in marriage. She will not, she says, need to refer to any books for this as her own experience is enough to make her an authority. And very experienced she is too. She has been married five times and her only worry is that she might be a little too experienced for her own good. She knows that the Church prefers people to be virgins and she is certainly not that. She also knows that the Church prefers widows not to marry again and she has not obeyed that either. However, she points out that this is all merely 'preference'. God never said that people must be virgins, nor has she seen a maximum number of husbands stated anywhere so she must finally conclude that she is free to do exactly what she wants.

She has, in fact, wanted five husbands – most of them for their money. The first three were old men whom she led a merry dance. She scolded them and accused them and made them pay dearly before they could even touch her and meanwhile she got up to all sorts of things behind their backs. However, they loved her and she gave them some pleasure too. The fourth husband caused her more trouble. He took a lover and made her miserable but she paid him back. When he died she buried him cheaply and spent her time admiring her next husband at the funeral.

The Wife's fifth husband was called Jankyn. He was half her age and she loved him very much. She handed over all her property to him but even this did not please him. He constantly criticised her behaviour and told her stories about all the wicked women in history. All these stories were gathered together in his favourite book and one night, when she felt that she could endure his abuse no longer, the Wife tore three pages right out of it. Jankyn hit her so hard for this that she would remain deaf all her life. At first, however, he thought that he might even have killed her. Horrified, he promised to let her have her way in all things. He signed all the property over to her and allowed her to tell him what to do for the rest of his life. And so, she says, they never argued again.

Now that she has told us her life story, the Wife begins to tell her tale. A knight has raped a young virgin and must answer a riddle to save his life. He must find out what it is that women most desire. He finally meets an ugly old woman who tells him that what women really want is power over men. However, in return for this information, he must marry her. He lies in bed disgusted on their wedding night and is lectured by the old woman for his bad behaviour and inability to see that true gentility is nothing to do with social position. However, she then offers him a choice. She can either be an ugly but faithful wife, or else she can be beautiful but unfaithful. The knight finally says that he would like her to make the choice. Delighted that he has given the power to her, the old woman turns into a young, beautiful and faithful wife and they live happily ever after.

THE WIFE OF BATH'S PROLOGUE

The prologue consists of the non-stop chatter of the Wife of Bath with no actual divisions in the text. It can, however, be roughly divided into three main sections:

I. The Wife's defence of marriage
II. The Wife's description of her married life
III. Jankyn and the 'Book of Wicked Wives'

SECTION I   THE WIFE'S DEFENCE OF MARRIAGE

LINES 1–34   The Wife wonders if the Church would recognise her five marriages

The Wife bursts upon the scene and states her intention to speak of the woe that is in marriage. She herself has had five husbands, the first of them when she was only twelve years old. Each time she has been widowed and married again. But now she wonders if the Church would recognise all these marriages. Christ only ever attended one wedding in the Bible so maybe one wedding is all that anyone is entitled to have. But the Wife also knows the story of Noah's Flood where everyone was told to 'go forth and multiply'.

> The Wife immediately sets up a division between her 'experience' and male 'auctoritee'. Experience is the very first word of her prologue and yet all is not as it seems. She goes on to quote more learned authors than anyone else in *The Canterbury Tales*. This passage alone uses three biblical examples together with many hidden references to St Jerome (see Literary Background, on The Anti-Feminist Tradition). The Wife's slippery skill as an arguer is also in evidence (see Narrative Techniques). She knows that learned men 'glosen' the text and use long words like 'bigamie' and 'octogamie' to try to obtain their own way but the Wife is determined to have a straight answer to a straight question.

auctoritee written authority such as the Bible or the writings of the great philosophers
sith since
have ywedded bee have been married
onis once

Cane of Galilee Cana, where Christ performed his first miracle by changing water into wine at a wedding (John 2:1)

Herkne eek … nones also listen, look, what a sharp retort indeed

Samaritan the woman of Samaria who was married five times. Christ said to her, 'he whom you now have is not your husband' (John 4:7–18)

ilke same

axe ask

Yet herde I … diffinicioun but in all my life I have never heard anyone state exactly what the permitted number of husbands was

Men may … doun men can guess and interpret in every way

I woot, expres I know clearly

wexe increase   .

lete leave

octogamie marrying eight times

vileynie in reproach

LINES 35–58   **The Wife thinks she has biblical support for her marriages**

The Wife points out that there are many husbands and wives in the Bible. In fact, some of the greatest men in the Old Testament were not only married, they had many wives. At any rate, she has never seen an exact figure of permissible husbands mentioned anywhere. Who is to say, therefore, that five or more is not allowed?

The Wife uses a very literal approach (see Narrative Techniques) as defence against 'glosing' clerics. She successfully gives examples from the Bible of people whose marriages were blessed by God and who even had more than one wife. The image of the 'mirie fit' which 'daun Salomon' would have had on each of his 700 wedding nights is, however, a little too vivid. The Wife reduces him to a fourteenth-century squire and with a nudge and a wink wishes that she could 'be refresshed half so ofte as he'. To mention Solomon is a good point but too graphic a description of his love life may weaken her case. She is supposed to raise herself to his level not bring him down to hers (see Language and Style).

daun sir

Salomon King Solomon, who was said to have had 700 wives and 300 concubines (1 Kings 11:3)

trowe believe

leveful lawful

Which yifte what a gift

so wel was him on live such a good life he enjoyed

a Goddes half by God

brinne burn

shrewed Lameth cursed Lamech, the first bigamist (Genesis 4:19)

Abraham and **Jacob** revered figures of the Old Testament

LINES 59–114   The Wife admits that virginity may be a higher state than marriage but this does not mean that everyone must be a virgin

Alison knows very well that St Paul advises men and women to remain virgins. However, she seizes on the word 'advises' and points out that virginity is not 'commanded' anywhere in the Bible. Indeed, if God wants large numbers of virgins to honour him then someone will have to get married and produce children. Otherwise, the whole human race will die out and there will be no more virgins left to worship anyone. Virginity may be perfection but the Wife of Bath does not claim to be perfect. She compares virginity and marriage with the kinds of dishes a lord will have in his house: he will have some golden ones but he will also have many made of wood and the wooden ones will do the job just as well, if not so prettily.

The Wife considers the status of marriage as opposed to virginity (see Themes, on Marriage) and continues in her attempt to get to the literal truth. Like an expert debater, she concludes that she cannot find virginity 'comanded' anywhere. The passage contains several proverbs or sayings and many homely details. St Paul and God are merely 'Poul' and 'his maister'. The biblical comparison of virgins with golden vessels and wives with wooden ones (2 Timothy 2:20) becomes a simple matter of domestic economy. The Bible had associated the wooden ones with dishonour and youthful lust but in the Wife's hands the thought of a house with only golden dishes seems absurd. But Alison is willing to admit that virginity is golden.

Quoting Jerome she says that virginity is like a 'dart' or prize in a race which only the best will be able to win. At least, that may be what she is saying. Her 'Cacche whoso may, who renneth best lat see' is deeply ambiguous and allows for the possibility that the dart will be chasing the women rather than the other way round.

expres explicit

it is no drede there is no doubt

He seyde ... noon he said that he had no divine authority

Thanne hadde ... dede then, by doing so, he would have condemned marriage

yaf noon heeste gave no commandment

The dart ... virginitee the 'dart' or spear would have been the prize in a race. Therefore, virginity is a great prize but not everyone in the human race will be able to win it. Only the best will manage to outrun marriage and be virgins

But this word ... his might but this call to virginity does not apply to everyone, only to those whom God, through his power, chooses to give it

maide virgin

But natheless ... saide he wished that every person were just like him

nis but it is only

leve / Of indulgence permission. St Paul encouraged people to marry if they found that a life of chastity was too difficult for them

so nis it ... bigamie so it is no shame for me to marry again if my husband dies, and I should not be accused of bigamy

For peril ... t'assemble it is dangerous to bring fire and flax (i.e., women and men) together

freletee frailty, weakness, being unable to resist sexual desire

Freletee clepe ... chastitee Frailty I call it, unless he and she are willing to live together without having sex. This was recommended by St Paul (I Corinthians 7:5)

Thogh maidenhede ... bigamie Even if virginity is considered better than a widow marrying again

It liketh ... goost It pleases them (i.e., the virgins) to be pure in body and soul

tree wood

sondry wise different ways

a propre yifte a special talent

as him liketh shifte as he pleases to distribute them

And continence ... devocion and so is a vow not to have sex when it is for
religious reasons

foore footsteps

LINES 115–62   The Wife turns to human biology to support her
argument

The reproductive organs are the Wife's next piece of evidence. The
theologians say that these were invented so that the bladder could be
emptied and so that a male could be differentiated from a female. However,
the Wife knows that this cannot be the whole story. The Bible says that a
husband must 'pay his marriage debt' to his wife in bed. Therefore, sexual
organs must have a pleasurable purpose too. Saintly people may choose not
to use them this way, but virginity is a state of perfection, not the norm.
Virgins are compared to pure white bread (a great delicacy in the Middle
Ages) while married people are like brown barley bread. The first is
definitely preferable but barley bread will adequately feed the hungry. And
the Wife will do more than an adequate job as a married woman. If the
Bible requires a 'marriage debt' she will make sure that it is paid very often.

> The Wife continues to argue more or less successfully (see Textual
> Analysis – Text 1). A dichotomy is set up throughout the prologue
> and tale between the female body and male asceticism (denial of the
> flesh) and this whole passage seems to affirm life and the body. Even
> the miracle is about eating. God gave heavenly bread which
> 'refresshed many a man'. The line is reminiscent of Solomon, a man
> who was 'refresshed' very often back at line 38. The holy act and sex
> are therefore cheekily linked by the one word. Spurred on by the
> connection, the Wife declares that she will never be 'daungerous' but
> will be generous with her favours. And yet, sex is described through-
> out the passage in terms of trade and commerce (see Imagery).

Telle me ... generacion tell me also, for what purpose were the sexual organs
made

And of so ... ywroght and created by so perfectly wise a maker

Glose interpret scripture

wrothe angry

for office, and for ese for practical use (i.e., urinating) and for pleasure

engendrure procreation

dette the so-called 'marriage debt' which required a husband to have sex with his wife, and a wife with her husband

his sely instrument his blessed, simple tool

eek also

holde obliged

Thanne sholde ... no cure then people would think virginity was unimportant

breed of pured whete-sede fine white bread made from wheat

And lat ... barly-breed and let us married women be called rough barley bread

I nam not precius I am not fussy

daungerous grudging, not free with one's sexual favours

him list he pleases

I wol nat lette I will not stop

Which shal ... my thral who shall be both my debtor and my slave

propre own

Al this ... every deel I like this pronouncement very much

LINES 163–92   The Pardoner interrupts the Wife of Bath

Shocked by the Wife's revelations so far, the Pardoner interrupts. He says that he was about to marry but is now not so sure that it is a good idea. The Wife tells him to listen to the rest of her tale and the Pardoner politely begs her to continue and teach the young men her practices. She continues, but first asks the company not to be annoyed at what she is about to say as she is only speaking in fun.

A medieval pardoner worked for the Church, collecting donations from those sorry for their sins and anxious to find forgiveness. The system, however, was open to exploitation and the Pardoner is part of Chaucer's 'rogues' gallery'. His manhood is called into question throughout *The Canterbury Tales* and his talk of taking a wife is probably an empty boast. If so, it would continue the theme of male impotence. The Wife frequently taunts her celibate male adversaries in this way throughout the prologue. The Pardoner, however, supports her telling her tale. He addresses her as if she were a learned preacher, calling her 'Dame', a title she is not entitled to but happily accepts. And she in her turn promises, like a good preacher, 'ensamples mo than ten' (see Literary Background).

Up stirt ... that anon the Pardoner jumped up at once

What sholde ... wyf to-yeere why should I bring such terrible misery on myself? I had better not marry any wife this year

tonne barrel

savoure tasted

abroche open

Ptholomee Ptolemy, an ancient mathematician and astronomer

Almageste Ptolemy's famous work of astronomy

praktike practices

sith it may yow like since it may please you

fantasye. inclination or desire

As taketh ... to pleye do not take offence at what I have to say, for my intention is only to entertain

SECTION II   THE WIFE'S DESCRIPTION OF HER MARRIED LIFE

LINES 193–223   **The Wife describes her life with her first three husbands**

Of her five husbands, the first three were rich old men and allegedly 'good'. Financially secure and confident that they doted on her, the Wife treated each of these husbands the same: badly. By being quarrelsome and always eager to cause trouble she made sure that they were always careful to please her. They would bring her presents, let her have her own way and be grateful when she spoke to them nicely.

In this section of the Wife's prologue, Chaucer shifts his attention away from Jerome and focuses instead on Theophrastus (see Literary Background, on The Anti-Feminist Tradition). The misogynists classed all women together as bad and all wives as nothing but trouble. This dehumanising practice is exploited here by Chaucer. He turns the prejudice around so that the woman is in control and the men become indistinguishable, lumped together without even a name between them. We might pity the husbands but it makes us realise how unfairly women were normally treated.

As evere moote ... seye sooth I promise to tell the truth or may I never drink wine or ale again

Unnethe mighte ... statut holde they could scarcely uphold their end of the marriage debt

pardee by God

swinke work

And, by ... no stoor and, by my faith, I did not care about it

Me neded ... diligence I did not need to trouble myself any longer

That I ne ... hir love that I did not value their love

bisie hire evere in oon be constantly busy

hoolly in myn hond completely under my thumb

What sholde ... myn ese? why should I take care to please them, unless it was for my profit and pleasure

sette hem so a-werke worked them so hard

weilawey alas

The bacon ... at Dunmowe the bacon was not fetched for them, I can tell you, that some men win in Essex at Dunmow. This is a reference to the 'Dunmow Flitch', a side of bacon awarded to married couples who had not quarrelled or wished that they were single all year

fawe eager

chidde hem spitously scolded them without mercy

LINES 224–34   The Wife's advice on how to handle husbands

The Wife is about to embark on a lengthy account of marital trouble and how she handled it all. Her general techniques are summed up by these principles: lie, cheat and accuse them before they accuse you.

> Lying and cheating were things which the misogynists always accused women of doing. The Wife is, therefore, acting like the stereotypical shrew. Such bitter old hags were common in medieval literature (see Literary Background, on The Anti-Feminist Tradition [La Vieille]) and the Wife comes closest to being one here. Chaucer is making sure that our response to the Wife remains a complicated one and that we see the bad side as well as the good.

Now herkneth ... proprely now let me tell you how well I managed things

bere hem wrong on honde accuse them wrongfully

lyen lie

But if it ... misavise except when they act without consideration

if that she kan hir good if she knows what is good for her

Bere him ... is wood will convince him that the chough is mad. This is a reference to a medieval story: a talking bird tells his master that his wife has been having an affair. The wife is guilty but denies the charge and tells her husband that the bird is mad. She and her maid then simulate a thunderstorm around the bird's cage, keeping it awake with their crashing and 'lightning' bolts. When it tells its master the next day that it was kept up all night by the storm, the master assumes that the bird must be mad and refuses to believe it any more

Of hir assent with her agreement, i.e., the maid is a knowing accomplice

LINES 235–92   The Wife's accusations against her husbands, attack
being the best form of defence

Alison begins a catalogue of her favourite charges against her old husbands. She accused them of lecherous behaviour, of chasing after the neighbours and the servants and then unfairly being suspicious of her and her 'friend'. She also said that they would find fault with any woman: a poor woman would be considered a great expense to her husband; a rich woman would be thought to be too proud; a beautiful woman would be suspected of being unfaithful. And even a plain wife, she says, would be accused of wanting to leap like an eager spaniel on the nearest available man. These faults are hidden, however, from the man looking for a wife. He will carefully inspect and try out beforehand all the things he owns: chairs, basins, clothes, horses. But a wife is the only thing that he takes on untried and then regrets when he discovers her vices.

The imagery in this passage is very offensive to women. They are reduced to the level of animals which should be tried out before they are bought (see Imagery). And then they are reduced even further, being compared to pots, basins and stools. But we should remember that the husbands did not in fact say these things. We could, therefore, condemn the Wife of Bath for her deceit. And yet, the insults are very vivid. The old husbands may not be guilty but some man somewhere is. In fact, this passage comes from the work of Theophrastus (see Literary Background) and was written to condemn women. The Wife is beating her husbands about the head with a weapon originally designed to hurt her, so can we really blame her for using it? It is a great reversal and one which also undermines Theophrastus. If he said these things and not the husbands then that makes him the 'olde dotard shrewe' (see Narrative Techniques, on Undermining the Enemy).

Sir olde kaynard ... array? sir old dotard, is this what you are up to?

over al ther wherever

I have no thrifty clooth I don't have a thing to wear

rowne whisper

gossib close friend, confidant

with ivel preef bad luck to you

To wedde ... for costage to marry a poor woman, on account of the expense

heigh parage high birth

holour lecher

gentillesse and daliaunce fine manners and flirtatious ways

It may so ... overal it is constantly attacked from every side

hire to chepe to do business with her

Ne noon ... withoute make there is no goose so grey in the lake, you say, that she does not want a mate, i.e., everyone wants a lover no matter how they look

welde control

A thing ... helde a thing that no man would willingly possess

lorel scoundrel

Ne no man ... hevene nor any man who hopes to go to heaven

With wilde ... tobroke with wild thunderbolt and fiery lightning, may your withered neck be broken to pieces

dropping dripping, leaky

What eyleth ... to chide? what is wrong with an old man that he would scold like this?

Til we be fast until we are securely married

assayed at diverse stoundes tried out at different times

Bacins, lavours ... hem bye basins, wash bowls, before men pay for them

But folk ... assay but people do not try out the women they intend to marry

LINES 293–307   The Wife accuses her husbands of accusing her

The next catalogue is a list of things of which the Wife accused her husbands of unfairly accusing her. These include the charge that she would become angry unless she were constantly flattered. Or that she would be annoyed if a fuss were not made over her birthday, or if any of her acquaintances, family or even servants were not treated with respect. She also claimed to be innocent of the suspicion that she was interested in the clerk, Jankyn.

> This passage is also traditional misogyny though the Wife gives it her individual touch. She would not have had so many servants and the reference to her father's 'allies' sounds unduly grand. The Wife clearly has a vain streak (she has already responded well to the Pardoner calling her 'dame'). The passage ends on a supreme note of **irony** as the Wife defends herself against her husband's suspicions about Jankyn: 'I wol him noght, thogh thou were deed tomorwe!'

But if that thou wolt unless you will
poure alwey constantly gaze
clepe call
make me fressh and gay make me feel young and attractive
norice nurse
And to my ... bour and to my chambermaid in my bedchamber
for his crispe heer because of his curly hair
squiereth me bothe up and doun escorts me everywhere
I wol him noght I would not have him

LINES 308–61   Alison points out the uselessness of trying to keep a
                wife prisoner

The Wife demands the keys to her husbands' treasure chests saying they can have control of their money or her body but not both. But in fact she has no intention of letting them control either. She says they should send her out to enjoy herself; after all, if another man lights his candle at her lantern, she will still shine just as brightly for her husband. Why should he care who has sex with his wife so long as *he* still does? And spying on her is not going to help. She will dress up and go 'caterwauling' when she pleases.

The Wife's desire for freedom is the theme of this passage but it is clear that her husbands have no real chance of tying her down. She talks outrageously about men lighting their 'candles' at her 'lantern'. At some points in her prologue she claims she was always faithful to her husbands, while at others she seems to be claiming the exact opposite (see Narrative Techniques, on Ambiguity and Irony). However, she moves us swiftly on and the section ends with a characteristic jumbling together of St Paul, a singed cat and a classical reference to the many-eyed Argus.

why hidestow why do you hide
What, wenestow ... dame? do you intend to have the lady of the house treated like an idiot?
wood mad
good property
That oon ... thine yen You're going to lose one of them, in spite of all your watchfulness
Taak youre disport ... talis have fun, I won't listen to any gossip about you
at oure large free to act as we please
Of alle men ... in honde the wisest man never cares who has the world under his control, i.e., the wise man is the one who is content with what he has, not caring who has more than he
queynte my 'pleasing thing', though the word borders on the obscene
werne refuse
Have thou ynogh ... pleyne thee if you have enough then you don't have any reason for complaint
thou most enforce thee you have to drive the point home
perree jewels
rubriche rubric, a guiding quote from the Bible
senge singe
Thanne wolde ...in his in then the cat would happily remain in his own house
goon a-caterwawed go caterwauling, i.e., looking for a mate
borel literally 'clothes' but possibly a euphemism
Argus the hundred-eyed guard of the ancient gods
warde-cors bodyguard
but me lest unless it pleases me
Yet koude I ... I thee I could deceive him, you had better believe it

LINES 362–402   **The Wife tells how she triumphed over her old husbands**

Alison reports the things that her old husbands said while they were drunk. She says that they compared a woman's love to hell, barren land, unquenchable fire and the worms which destroy a tree. This is all false but she calls Jankyn and her niece as witnesses. Her innocent husbands are so busy defending themselves that they cannot accuse her. And, anyway, perhaps they were a little bit pleased to find her so 'jealous' and willing to believe they had been with other women when they could really barely stand up.

> This passage contains many misogynist images of women (see Textual Analysis – Text 2) together with an account of some of the Wife's most blatant deceit. In the light of both of these things it is surprising that men and women should ever manage to live together at all. But the tone is lightened by the Wife's lively style as she tells how she 'tikled' her husbands' hearts nevertheless. It is a touching choice of verb. However, in the light of the passage as a whole, poking their hearts with a sharp stick might seem a more adequate description.

And that no ... ferthe and that no man could endure the fourth thing
leeve dear
Been ther ... resemblances is there no other kind of comparison
But if a sely ... tho? but an innocent wife has to be one of them
liknest compare
wilde fyr Greek fire, a highly flammable mixture used in warfare
shende destroy
Baar I ... on honde I firmly swore to my old husbands
Ful giltelees even though they were completely innocent
I koude ... the gilt I knew how to complain even though I was the one in the wrong
spilt ruined
grint grinds. A medieval variant of 'first come, first served'
blive quickly
never agilte hir live they were never guilty in their lives
Of wenches ... on honde I would accuse them of having mistresses
for sik unnethes mighte they stonde they were so ill they could scarcely stand

Wende that I ... chiertee thought that I had such great love for him
dighte copulated with
colour pretence
kindely naturally

LINES 403–30   The Wife makes her husbands pay

The Wife boasts that she always came off best in the end. She did not want the advances of her old husbands but would tolerate them in bed for a price. However, she would never tolerate any criticism and any cross word was paid back to her husbands with interest.

The passage shows the Wife talking like a professional rhetorician (see Literary Background) and also like a businesswoman. Her love life with her husbands is described in terms of trade and commerce (see Imagery) but she reveals that there was a more emotional side to her character. She confesses, with considerable insight, that it was her sexual distaste for these old men which made her 'chide' them so often. She is like a hawk with no taste for 'old meat' (bacon). She mocks their feeble efforts in bed, dismissing their attempts at 'nicetee' or 'silly business'. In the end, after all the mockery and arguments, each old husband is 'as a wood leon'. But we should notice not just that she has made them mad, more importantly she has made them look like lions – the symbol for women in the prologue (see Imagery). The Wife has redressed the balance and taken away men's natural advantage. However, it is only temporary. They only 'looked' like lions.

I avaunte me I boast
the bettre in ech degree the advantage in all respects
Namely abedde ... meschaunce in bed, especially, they had a miserable time
do hem no plesaunce give them no pleasure
raunson ransom
suffre hym do his nicetee allow him to do his 'silly business'
haukes hawks
For winning ... endure I would endure his lust in order to make money
bacon old meat, i.e., her old husbands
hadde seten hem biside had sat down beside them
bord table

I quitte hem I paid them back
yeve it up give it up
a wood leon a mad lion
faille of his conclusion not get his way

LINES 431–51 The Wife uses the men's arguments against them

Alison points out to her husbands that someone has to give in if they are
going to live in peace. And since a man is so much more reasonable than a
woman, she says, the man should give in more easily. Then she teases him
that if she were to sell herself she would do very well but her 'pretty thing'
is for him alone.

The Wife is exploiting male and female stereotypes here (see
Character, on Female Stereotypes). She is using men's image of
themselves as reasonable and superior against them. If women are so
stupid and emotional then 'clever' men should just let them win. Of
course, this argument shows the Wife at her cleverest.

Goode lief, taak keep sweetheart, take note
How mekely … sheep! how meek our sheep, Willie, looks. The Wife is
encouraging her husband to take the docile sheep as a role model
lat me ba thy cheke let me kiss your cheek. 'Ba' would be a word used to
children
spiced scrupulous
Jobes pacience the patience of Job. Having endured all the torments God
could devise for him, Job's patience was legendary
it is fair to have a wyf in pees it is a fine thing to live with a wife in peace
ye moste been suffrable you are more able to bear suffering
Is it for ye wolde … queynte allone? is it because you want my sexual favours
all to yourself
Peter! by St Peter!
bele chose pretty thing. Another of the Wife's euphemisms

LINES 452–502 The Wife tells of her fourth husband

The Wife remembers her youth and how full of vitality and passion she
was. She would dance and sing, drink and make love (the making love
being apparently an inevitable effect of the drink). Her youth has passed

but she has no regrets. Her fourth husband, however, is not altogether a happy memory. He was unfaithful to her and she was jealous. As a result she tried to make his life miserable and no doubt succeeded. But now he is dead, buried in a cheap tomb.

The Wife's triumphant mastery of her first three husbands gives way now to the more melancholy atmosphere of the fourth. Old women in medieval literature often show bitterness and hatred when they remember their past (see Literary Background, on The Anti-Feminist Tradition [La Vieille]), but the Wife has no regrets. Her optimism is one of her great qualities and it triumphs here. Alison becomes less of a one-dimensional figure. She is still full of energy and spirit but she shows grace in the way she accepts the passing of her youth and a softer, more vulnerable side – for a few moments anyway.

paramour lover
ragerie passion
pie magpie
cherl churl, villain
birafte his wyf hir lyf deprived his wife of her life, i.e., murdered her
thogh although if
daunted frightened
For al so ... likerous tail for as surely as cold gives rise to hail, a greedy mouth goes with a greedy tail
In wommen ... no defence drunken women cannot defend their honour
boote good
envenime poison
Hath me biraft ... pith has taken away my beauty and my vigour
bren bran
But he was quit ... Joce! but he was paid back, by God and St Judocus!
of the same wode a croce a cross of the same wood
Nat of my body not by committing adultery
I made folk swich cheere I was so friendly to everyone
grece grease
purgatorie purgatory. A place of suffering where the souls of the dead waited until they were pure enough to enter heaven
wrong pinched
deyde died

And lith ... beem and lies buried under the rood beam, i.e., in the cheaper part of the church

curius intricate

As was the ... wroghte subtilly as was the sepulchre (tomb) of that man Darius, which Apelles skilfully made. Darius was the warrior king of the Persians. Apelles was a celebrated craftsman of the time

It nis but wast it would only have been a waste

cheste coffin

LINES 503–24   **The Wife tells of the violence of husband number five and of her love for him nevertheless**

Alison begins this section with an appeal to God to protect the soul of her fifth husband, Jankyn. And yet he was the cruellest of the five and the Wife still bears the scars of his violence. He was standoffish with her but this only made her desire him more – such is the perverse nature of women, she says.

The Wife finally finds a man to whom she wants to submit. Significantly he is 'fressh' in bed but even more significant is his ability to 'glose' the Wife and get his way. Alison has been so proud of herself up until now, always able to overcome male 'glosing', but now she surrenders. Worse, the verbal abuse of the 'glosing' male writers becomes physical abuse from Jankyn.

al by rewe one after another

so wel koude he me glose he knew so well how to get round me

bete beaten

trowe believe

daungerous standoffish, hard to get

queynte fantasye (pun) quaint fantasy, to do with women's private parts

Waite what ... crave whatever thing we may not easily have, we will cry for and crave all day

Preesse on us faste pursue us closely

With daunger ... chaffare we lay out the goods we have to sell sparingly

Greet prees ... litel prys many buyers at the market make the prices high. Something sold too cheaply will not be valued at all

LINES 525–85   **The Wife relates how she met Jankyn while her fourth husband was still alive**

One Lent, while her fourth husband was in London, the Wife spent a good deal of time at the home of her friend, a woman also named Alison. She gossiped, told her husband's private business and flirted with her friend's lodger, a young Oxford scholar named Jankyn. She even told him that if she were a widow again she would marry him. After all, she says, a woman should always think of these things in advance: a woman with only one man is in as much trouble as a mouse with only one hole to run to.

She also told him that she had had a dream where he killed her, covering her bed in blood. But she invents this only so that she can speak about her wealth, as blood is interpreted as gold in dream lore. Thus, flaunting her gold, she hopes to attract him to her, not because of his wealth this time, but because she wants his love.

> Jankyn is a 'clerk' which links him broadly with Jerome and the anti-female tradition. On the other side we have Alison and her friend 'Alisoun'. It is strange that Chaucer should have chosen the same name for the friend. Indeed, 'oure apprentice Janekin' at line 303 may be a different man from Jankyn the 'clerk'. Chaucer may be dividing men and women into two broad camps. This is not just the life story of Alison of Bath, it is about the battle between 'Jankyns' and 'Alisons', between men and women. Her tale makes the same point. There none of the main characters are named at all.

clerk scholar

wente at hom to bord became a boarder in the house

gossib close friend

privetee secrets

biwreyed revealed

conseil business

in a Lente during Lent

leyser leisure, opportunity

eek for to be seye also to be seen

Of lusty folk by pleasure loving people

what wiste I wher my grace how could I know where my love

Was shapen for to be was destined to be

vigilies vigils, gatherings on the night before a religious holiday

pleyes of miracles miracle plays, religious but very popular drama

And wered ... scarlet gites and wore my gay scarlet red clothes

frete hem never a deel didn't eat holes in them at all

daliance flirtation

purveiance foresight, future plans

widwe widow

bobance boast

sterte run

mette dreamed

LINES 586–602   Husband number Four dies but the Wife has already picked out Jankyn as his replacement

Alison's fourth husband dies conveniently quickly and she is free to pursue Jankyn, even at the funeral. She makes a great show of grief but her widow's veil allows her secretly to admire Jankyn's shapely legs as he follows the coffin. The Wife is in love for the first time, with a man literally half her age.

> Chaucer now stops using chunks of literature from his anti-female sources and tells a slightly more individual story about the Wife. The battle stops momentarily as she speaks of her genuine feeling for this man.

on beere on his bier

algate continuously

mooten must

coverchief cloth for covering the head

But for that ... a make but because I had already provided myself with a new husband

but smal only a little

born a-morwe carried the next morning

so clene and faire so shapely and attractive

a coltes tooth the tooth of a young horse, i.e., youthful desires

LINES 603–26   The Wife's horoscope

Alison digresses again to tell how her personality was influenced by the stars. As a Taurean she was born under the power of Venus but warlike Mars was also situated in Taurus at this time. As a result she is pleasure loving and promiscuous and has a bold and unstoppable nature. As such, she could never deny a man her 'chamber of Venus' no matter what he looked like or how poor he was. After all, she had often been told that she had the best 'thingummebob' imaginable and if a man was willing to admire then the Wife was willing to be generous.

However, we have only a glimpse of this vulnerable, loving Wife before she disappears behind a stereotype again. This time it is her horoscope (see Character, on Astronomy and Physiognomy). In spite of her earlier protestations that she was always faithful to her husbands she now tells us that she always followed her 'appetit' and loved any type of man 'that he liked me', a dangerously ambiguous claim (see Narrative Techniques, on Ambiguity and Irony).

Gat-tothed with teeth set wide apart

I hadde ... Venus seel I bore the imprint of St Venus's mark. The Wife has a birthmark which she claims is due to her being born under the planetary influence of Venus. Venus was the ancient goddess of love and would never have been a candidate for sainthood

wel bigon in a good situation, having inherited the wealth of the last four husbands

quoniam whatsit: an innocent Latin word but the Wife is using it euphemistically for her genitalia

I am al Venerien in feelinge I am dominated by Venus when it comes to my emotions, i.e., always ready to fall in love

myn herte is Marcien my heart is dominated by the planet Mars. Mars was the ancient god of war

Venus me yaf ... hardinesse Venus gave me my sexual desire and lustfulness, and Mars gave me my obstinate bold nature

ascendent was Taur sign of the zodiac was Taurus, the bull

constellacioun horoscope

chambre of Venus another euphemism but it is not difficult to guess where 'Venus's room' would be on the Wife's body

Martes mark Mars's mark, another birthmark or else the Wife's very red complexion

privee private, secret

For God ... savacioun for, as God is my salvation

discrecioun moderation

SECTION III   JANKYN AND THE 'BOOK OF WICKED WIVES'

LINES 627–65   **Jankyn and the Wife are now married but he objects to her behaviour**

Within the month, Alison has married Jankyn and signed over all her property to him as an act of love. He, however, is not so pleased with her. He wants her to stop going on pilgrimages, stop going from house to house gossiping, and generally stop all her past behaviour. He beats her when she tears a page from his book and is constantly quoting stories to her about husbands who left their wives because the wives would not do as they were told.

The Wife now has to suffer the 'wo' in marriage which up until now she has caused. She has previously been at more of a distance from the anti-women literature and has also used it as a weapon against men. Now she must endure the barrage of misogyny which Jankyn heaps upon her.

hende nice, courteous, clever
with greet solempnitee with great ceremony and celebration
fee property
He nolde ... my list he would not grant me any of my desires
he smoot me ones on the list he hit me once on the ear
rente tore
Stibourn stubborn
jangleresse chatterbox
although he had it sworn even though he had sworn that I should not
olde Romain geestes tales of ancient Rome
he Simplicius Gallus that man Simplicius Gallus
Noght but ... hir say only because he saw her bareheaded
That, for his wyf ... hire eke who, because his wife was at midsummer festival without his knowledge, also left her
Ecclesiaste Ecclesiasticus 25.25 'Do not allow water to flow freely, nor a wicked woman freedom to gad about'
roule about gad about
salwes willow branches
And priketh ... the falwes and spurs his blind horse across the open fields
to go seken halwes to go on pilgrimages

galwes gallows

I sette noght an hawe I didn't give a berry, i.e. I didn't care a bit

sawe saying

Ne I wolde ... corrected be nor would I allow myself to be corrected by him

wood al outrely completely angry

I nolde ... in no cas I could not submit to him at all

LINES 666–710   **The Wife tells of Jankyn's favourite book and criticises the men who write such stories**

Alison now tells us more about the book she tore. Jankyn had a book which he would read whenever he had a spare moment. It was a collection of some of the best known authors of the Middle Ages – all of them telling stories which condemned women. Alison hated this book of 'wicked wives' and despised the male scholars who wrote it. These old men, she says, do not understand women but they are the ones who write all the stories. If women were doing the writing there would be plenty of tales to tell about men!

All the authors whom the Wife has been fighting against and twisting in her own defence now appear in person. Jankyn's 'book of wikked wives' is a collection of all the best known anti-female writers of the Middle Ages. It is as if the Wife has been shadow boxing until now but has lost her appetite for the fight when someone gets into the ring with her. She carries on, however, and demands to know who 'peyntede the leon'. It is a key question because it points out that medieval women existed in a world where everything – art, literature, religion, work, family life – was controlled by men.

by Seint Thomas the pilgrims are travelling to the shrine of St Thomas à Becket at Canterbury. He was a bishop murdered in his own cathedral by the king's men in 1170

desport amusement

He cleped ... Theofraste he called it Valerius and Theophrastus. Both of these are anti-marriage texts

Jerome St Jerome (AD341–420) a famous scholar known for his strict lifestyle and harsh views on women and sexuality

a book again Jovinian Jovinian was a monk who said that marriage was equal to virginity in the eyes of God. Jerome wrote a book attacking him

Tertulan Tertullian, an early Christian who wrote in praise of chastity, modesty and monogamy

Crisippus condemned by St Jerome for suggesting that people ought to marry

Trotula a female physician, expert on the bodies and ways of women

Helowis Heloïse. She secretly married her tutor, the scholar Abelard. He was castrated by her angry family and lived out the rest of his life as a priest. She became prioress of a convent near Paris

Ovides Art a book on love by the Roman author Ovid

He knew of hem ... Bible he knew more legends and biographies of them than of good women in the Bible

an impossible an impossibility

never the mo in any way

Who peyntede ... who? the lion's question when he saw a picture of a man killing a lion. Had a lion painted the picture, then the roles would have been reversed

withinne hire oratories in their chapels

Mercurie Mercury, ruling planet of intellectuals and scholars

Been in hir ... contrarius are completely different in their outlook

riot and dispence debauchery and extravagant living

And, for hire ... exaltacioun the planets are opposites and so Venus is at her weakest when Mercury is most powerful and vice versa

desolat powerless

kan nat kepe hir mariage cannot stay faithful to their marriage vows

LINES 711–87   **The Wife gives examples of some of the terrible stories Jankyn read her from his book**

Jankyn does not just read his book, he insists on reading it aloud to Alison. He tells the story of Eve, who ate the apple in the Garden of Eden. For this, he says, Jesus Christ himself was killed and all humanity suffered. This, however, is only the beginning of a long list of wives who betrayed, humiliated, and murdered their husbands. Some wives managed all three together, murdering their husbands and having sex with a lover while the corpse lay on the floor. Some preferred merely to drive nails into their husband's brain.

The catalogue of 'wicked women' is lengthy but Chaucer is using only a fraction of the stories he could have used. Nevertheless, the Wife and the audience have had enough. Some of the horrors are memorable but the most memorable lines of all are the Wife's final summation: 'Who wolde wene, or who wolde suppose,/ The wo that in myn herte was, and pine?' She no longer wants to deal in misogynist stereotypes.

oure sire the head of the household

Eva according to the Bible, Eve ate the apple that the serpent offered her and offered it to Adam too. They and their descendants were then banished from Paradise

expres clearly

Sampson in the Bible, Samson was betrayed by Delilah who cut off his hair and made him weak so that his enemies could blind him

lemman lover

Hercules in Greek legend, Deianira gave her husband Hercules a magic shirt which she thought would win back his love. In fact, it was poisoned and he burned himself alive to escape the pain

Socrates a Greek philosopher whose scholarly life was said to have been disrupted by marriage trouble

Er that thonder ... a reyn rain has to fall before the thunder will stop

Phasipha Pasiphae had sex with a bull and gave birth to the Minotaur, part bull and part man

shrewednesse wickedness

Clitermystra Clytemnestra murdered her husband Agamemnon in his bath with an axe

Amphiorax Amphiaraus. His wife Eriphyle was bribed with a necklace to convince him to take part in a battle. He took her advice and died

ouche brooch

Livia poisoned her husband at the instigation of her lover

Lucia Lucia accidentally poisoned her husband with a too-powerful love potion

algates always

for herte despitus out of bitterness of heart

dighte hire copulate with her

upright face upwards

usinge for to chide constantly nagging

They haten ... loven ay they always hate whatever gives their husbands pleasure

cast of hir smok takes off her clothes
but she be chaast also unless she is also chaste
wene imagine

LINES 788–810 Furious, the Wife tears at the book but Jankyn knocks her down

Thinking that the stories will never stop, Alison tears three pages from the book and hits Jankyn so hard in the face that he tumbles into the fire. At once, he leaps up and strikes Alison with his fist and she lies on the floor as if dead. Horrified, Jankyn rushes to her. 'Have you murdered me for my land?' asks the Wife. 'Never mind, I must have one last kiss.' Jankyn bends down to kiss her and the Wife hits him again.

The tearing of Jankyn's book is a symbolic gesture. The Wife had used anti-female literature against her first husbands and had it used against her by Jankyn, now the only way forward is for it all to be destroyed. The Wife has moved away from the stereotypes and in the end we see them going up in flames. But we should not believe in peace and harmony just yet. The Wife is still the Wife (and characteristically increases the torn pages from one to three in this final section) and still needs to triumph. She wants to love Jankyn but before she does so she wants to deal him, and all male domination, a healthy blow in the face.

fine stop
plight plucked
radde was reading
I with my … cheke I gave him such a blow on the cheek with my fist
up stirte as dooth a wood leoun jumped up like a mad lion
wolde han fled his way would have run away
out of my swogh I breyde I came round from my faint
mordred murdered
suster sister, in the sense that they are part of the same church
That I have doon … to wite you have yourself to blame for what I have done
and that I thee biseke I beg you most sincerely
eftsoones immediately
thus muchel am I wreke I take this much revenge

LINES 811–28   **The Wife and Jankyn are reconciled**

In spite of unfair tactics, Alison and Jankyn are finally reconciled. Jankyn burns his book and gives control of the household and property back to Alison. She also demands control of everything that he says and does and has him declare that she can do whatever she wants for the rest of her life. After that, they never had another argument.

> The fire, which had been an anti-women image throughout the prologue, finally gets to consume the misogynists as all their writing goes symbolically up in smoke. With the stereotypical images of women now out of the way, the Wife and Jankyn should be able to live together honestly and happily. Indeed, we are told that from that day on they never had another argument. But this seems to have been achieved at some cost to Jankyn who has to surrender not only control of the house and land but even his very 'tonge' to Alison. However, she in her turn is 'to him as kinde/ As any wyf from Denmark unto Inde'. It seems like a fair arrangement but the more cynical may remember that 'kinde' means two things in the Middle Ages: 'kind' and 'according to one's nature'. If it is true that she was 'kind' to Jankyn then it is a happy ending. But if it means that she followed the 'kinde' of women (which was defined in lines 401–2 as 'deceit, sorrow, spinning') then the old issues are still not resolved.

We fill … selven two we came to an agreement between the two of us
hond hand
brenne his book anon right tho burn his book there and then
maistrie mastery
soverainetee control, supremacy
Do as thee lust do as you please
Keep thyn … myn estaat guard your honour and also my standing in society
debaat argument
And also trewe and just as faithful

LINES 829–56   **The Friar interrupts and argues with the Summoner**

The Friar laughs when he realises that the Wife has only reached the end of her prologue and is still to tell her tale. This angers the Summoner who compares the interfering Friar to a fly buzzing at every dish, unable to mind his own business. The Host intervenes to stop them arguing and asks the Wife to continue with her tale which she agrees to do, if the Friar will permit it.

Jankyn's anti-female book has been burned, but in case we thought that was the end of it, Chaucer now has the Friar laugh at the Wife of Bath. The Friar is a man of the church and a traditional enemy of women in the Middle Ages. The battle therefore continues. The Summoner comes to the Wife's defence but more because he hates friars than supports the Wife. And, anyway, he is another of Chaucer's rogues – diseased, drunken and corrupt. If Chaucer had wanted to defend the Wife he could have given her a better champion than this. But, then again, the Wife is quite capable of defending herself, as her tale shows.

lough laughed
preamble preface, introduction
Somonour Summoner, someone who worked for the Church courts and summoned people to appear before the tribunal
gale cry out
Goddes armes two! by God's two arms, an oath
entremette hym interfere
Wol falle in every dissh likes to drop into every dish
What! amble ... sit doun! why, go amble yourself, or trot, or be quiet or go sit down. The Summoner does not know what 'preamble' is but thinks it must be something to do with 'amble', an easy pace on horseback
Thou lettest oure disport you are spoiling our fun
Ye, woltow so So, is that how you want it?
bishrewe curse
But if unless
Sidingborne Sittingbourne. A town forty miles from London and a likely stopping point on the road to Canterbury
morne mourn
Ye fare as ... of ale you're acting like people drunk on ale
licence permission

LINES 857–81   **The Wife discusses the demise of the fairies and the rise of the friars as a danger to women**

Once upon a time in the reign of King Arthur, says the Wife, the land was inhabited by fairies. Now, however, the friars have driven them away and where one would have encountered an elf before there is now only a friar. Or rather, many friars, for they are as thick on the ground as specks of dust in a sunbeam. Women can now travel without fear of fairy lovers. The only trouble they will meet on the road now will be a friar and he will only dishonour them.

> The Wife begins by taking revenge on the Friar. As a man of God he should have been holy but friars had a reputation for being greedy and lecherous. His 'blessinge' sounds more than a little intrusive as the Wife compiles a large, too large, list of the places he is likely to visit, including people's bedrooms. He becomes equated with the incubi or demon-lovers of fairy stories. The theme of aggressive male sexuality is therefore set up, ready for the rape in the next section.

King Arthour   King Arthur, legendary king of Britain
fulfild of faierie   filled with fairies
elf-queene   fairy queen
mede   meadow
limitours   friars who were licensed to work within a certain 'limit' or area
motes   specks of dust
boures   bedrooms
burghes   boroughs, towns
Thropes, bernes ... daieries   villages, barns, stables, dairies
For ther ... an elf   for in the places where a fairy used to walk
undermeles and in morweninges   late mornings (nine to twelve) and mornings
saufly   safely
incubus   an evil spirit believed to copulate with sleeping women
And he ne wol ... dishonour   and he will only dishonour them

LINES 881–918   **A knight rapes a young woman and must answer a question correctly to save his life**

A knight encounters a maiden and rapes her. He is then captured and taken to Arthur's court to be put to death. However, the queen and her ladies intervene and beg for him to be handed over to them. They then set him a test: to find out what it is that women most desire, or else face the death penalty. The knight accepts the challenge and promises to return within the year with his answer.

The rape, one of Chaucer's additions to the old story (see Literary Background) is described very casually as though it is entirely natural that the woman should have been attacked in this way. It is an extreme example of the way in which women were often regarded as less than human or as mere property (see Imagery). But this is no fourteenth-century court and the knight faces the death sentence. His offence has been against women but **ironically** the women step in to save his life. However, it is not out of compassion. They want him to be placed in the same powerless position as women usually are, with the fate of his body in someone else's hands.

bacheler young knight

as he was born as he rode

maugree hir heed against her will

rafte hire maidenhed took away her virginity

oppressioun rape

dampned condemned

Paraventure swich ... statut tho perhaps that was the law at that time

preyeden the king of grace begged the king to show mercy

spille put to death

in swich array in such trouble

suretee certainty, security

keep thy nekke-boon from iren! keep the axe from your neck

to seche and leere to search and learn

suffisant satisfactory

Thy body ... in this place to give yourself up in this place, i.e., at the end of the year

purveye provide

LINES 919–82   **The knight is offered many answers to his question**

The knight sets off and asks many people what it is that women most desire but each answer he hears is different from the last. Some say that women desire riches, others say a good time, some say nice clothes, others sexual pleasure. The Wife herself knows that women like to be flattered and courted and that none of them ever like to be told they have a fault, even if they have many. And as for the suggestion that women most desire to keep secrets, the Wife finds that a ridiculous notion.

All the answers here could have come straight out of the Wife's prologue. They reduce women to silly creatures, easily swayed by presents and flattery. But the strange thing is, the Wife declares that they come 'ful ny the sothe'. Even worse, she tells the story of Midas whose wife could not keep the secret of his ass's ears. But this is not true. It was Midas's barber who told the world about his ears. Alison has therefore made women look bad by telling a story which falsely condemns wives. It is an example once more of the Wife's complicated character and a reminder that she cannot just be viewed as a noble defender of women. Or perhaps the analysis can be taken to a deeper level. As the audience laughs at the woman who 'as a bitore bombleth in the mire', the Wife refers them to Ovid for the rest of the story. Anyone eager enough to look it up would find the culprit was in fact a man. And so the joke would not be quite what they thought it was. It might in fact be on them.

he ne koude arriven in no coost he could not discover any place
accordinge in-feere agreeing together
he gooth ful ny the sothe he comes very close to the truth
bisinesse attentive service
Been we ylimed ... lesse we are caught, rich women and poor alike
right as us lest just as we please
repreve us tell us off
no thing nice not at all silly
If any wight ... sooth if any man should touch us on a sore spot, that we will not lash out on being told the plain truth about ourselves
Assay try it
We wol ... of sinne we want to be considered wise and without any faults
stable, and eek secree constant and able to keep a secret
biwreye reveal, betray
rake-stele rake handle
Pardee ... thing hele in faith, we women can keep nothing secret
Mida Midas, the king of ancient legend whose touch turned everything to

gold. He was also famous for his ass's ears, set upon him by the gods when he judged wrongly in a musical contest. His story was told by the Roman poet Ovid

heres hair

That, save his wyf ... namo so that, apart from his wife, no one else knew about them

But nathelees ... conseil hide but nevertheless, she thought that she would die if she had to keep a secret for so long

swal swelled

That nedely ... moste asterte that of necessity some word must escape her

mareys marsh

as a bitore bombleth as a bittern (a type of wading bird) booms

leere learn

LINES 983–1045   An old woman gives the knight the answer but in return he must grant her one request

At the end of the year the knight still does not have an answer to the question, but as he rides back to Arthur's court he encounters an old woman in a forest. She is uglier than anyone could ever imagine but in desperation he asks her for her help. She agrees to give him the answer but in return he must grant her one request. The knight agrees to the bargain and they travel together to the court where the ladies have already assembled. 'What women most desire', says the knight, 'is to have mastery over men'. The court agrees and the knight's life is saved.

> The knight approaches the fairy dancers 'In hope that som wisdom sholde he lerne'. In fact, this is exactly what is going to happen. In Chaucer's sources the knight only learns the answer to the riddle. In *The Wife of Bath's Tale* the knight is going to learn far more – he is going to learn about women, about love and about humanity. 'Sovereinetee' and 'maistrie' are by now familiar terms. This is exactly what the Wife achieved at the end of her prologue with Jankyn (line 818).

goost spirit

sojourne remain

ful yerne very eagerly

he niste where he did not know where

Again the knight ... gan rise the old woman rose to meet the knight

heer forth ne lith no wey go no further

kan muchel thing know many things

I nam but ... seyn I am a dead man unless I am able to say

Koude ye ... youre hire If you could inform me, I would pay you very well for your trouble

Plight me thy trouthe pledge me your word

avante boast

calle a hairnet worn as a headdress

Tho rowned ... his ere then she whispered a message in his ear

hight promised

bode appeere commanded to appear

This knight ... a best this knight did not stand still like a dumb animal

that contraried that who disagreed with

LINES 1046–1108   The old woman now makes her request – the knight must take her as his wife

The old woman now demands that the knight keep his part of the bargain. She has saved his life and now he must marry her. The knight is devastated and begs her to make a different request but the woman stands firm. Disgusted and humiliated, the knight marries her and takes her to his bed for their wedding night. He turns away from her in revulsion and is chastised by the woman but he cannot accept her ugliness, her old age or the fact that she is not of noble birth.

> In the sources the knights knew beforehand that they would have to marry the Loathly Lady in return for the answer to the riddle. Our knight does not know what the condition will be and is consequently placed in a far more vulnerable position. He is completely in the old woman's power, a reversal of the normal male female relationship. The 'lusty bacheler' (line 883) of the tale's opening now 'hidde him as an owle', no longer dominant and in control and far less inclined to be 'lusty'.

biheste promise

as chees a newe requeste make another request

That under ... lith above that is buried under the earth or lies above

But if thy wyf I were unless I were your wife

nacioun family, lineage
disparaged degraded
Constreyned forced, compelled
That for my ... no cure that out of carelessness I overlook
walweth writhes
dangerous standoffish, hard to get
unright injury, wrong
loothly loathsome, disgusting
comen of so lough a kinde descended from such low family
winde roll about
So wel ye ... unto me so that you would behave very well towards me

LINES 1109–76   The old woman lectures the knight on what nobility
really means

Nobility, says the old woman, is nothing to do with birth. A person is truly
noble only if their actions are good. Aristocratic ancestors can pass their
money down to us but not their virtue and without that we cannot be called
noble. A fire placed in the darkest home will not be consumed by the
darkness. Just so, true nobility will shine on regardless of poverty. If the son
of a duke does not behave in a virtuous fashion then nothing can make him
noble but anyone who lives virtuously is noble even if they come from the
poorest family.

> The Loathly Lady's speech on 'gentillesse' changes the tone of the
> tale. It is no longer a battle of women against men, it becomes a
> lecture on the worth of all humanity. Indeed, most of its material
> would have been familiar from medieval sermons. And a knight, of all
> people, ought to have known these things already. The concept of
> knighthood is built on 'gentillesse' and the duties of courtesy. The
> paradox is that our knight's mind has been fixed on lower things and
> it takes a lowly woman to remind him what the higher things are. The
> theme of reversal is once more in evidence.

gentillesse nobility
Privee and apert in private and in public
entendeth strives
heigh parage noble lineage
Dant Dante Alighieri (1265–1321), great Italian poet

Ful selde ... gentillesse   moral integrity rarely reaches all the way down the branches of the family tree; instead God, in his goodness, wants us to inherit our nobility from him

temporel   worldly

fine   cease

To doon ... faire office   to perform all the noble duties of a true gentleman

mount of Kaukasous   Caucasian mountains, i.e., a long way away

As twenty ... biholde   as it would if 20,000 men were watching it

genterie   nobility

annexed to   joined to

Sith folk ... in his kinde   since people do not always behave as they should, like the fire does, which acts according to its nature

nel himselven do no gentil dedis   will not do any noble deeds himself

For vileyns ... cherl   a man who acts like a low person is a low person. Villeins and churls were the lowest rank in medieval society

renomee   renown, reputation

bountee   goodness

Which is ... persone   which is nothing to do with you

It was no ... place   it was not bequeathed to us along with our place in society

Tullius Hostillius   legendary third king of Rome who began life as a herdsman

Senek and **Boece**   Seneca and Boethius, both philosophers

expres that it no drede is   clearly, it is beyond dispute

Al were it ... rude   although my ancestors were humble

weive synne   abandon sin

LINES 1177–216   The old woman lectures the knight on poverty and old age

As for her poverty, the old woman says, she should not be criticised for that. Christ himself chose to live in poverty after all. Anyone who is satisfied with their lot in life cannot be called poor. Only those who are always wanting something else can really be called poor. Poverty can bring misery but it also encourages people to work hard and lets them see God, themselves and their true friends more clearly.

As for old age, authors always say that this should be respected. Besides, she says, if a man has an ugly old wife then he should be pleased because there is no possibility that another man will want to sleep with her.

The Loathly Lady argues with the knight in a manner very reminiscent of the Wife's arguments in the prologue. Like the Wife she rejects 'auctoritee' and then uses it to support her arguments. But in a wider sense 'authority' has been rejected. The knight is male and part of the ruling class, 'authority' therefore belongs to him by right. But everything has been turned around. The knight has shown that he knows nothing and must be educated by his exact opposite, a woman without power.

repreeve reproach
wilful voluntary
Ne wolde nat ... living would not choose an immoral way of life
Whoso that halt him paid whoever feels content
sherte shirt
coveiteth covets, desires
Verray poverte ... proprely true poverty sings by its very nature, i.e., it is a happy way of life
Juvenal a Roman poet known for his sympathy with the poor
hateful good an unsought blessing
bringere-out of bisinesse an encouragement to work hard
A greet ... sapience also a great improver of wisdom
alenge miserable
Maketh his ... to knowe teaches him to know God and himself
spectacle a pair of glasses
verray true
an oold wight doon favour behave respectfully to the old
cokewold cuckold, a cheated husband
also moot I thee so may I prosper

LINES 1217–35   **The old woman offers to be a faithful but ugly wife or else beautiful and untrue. The knight lets her decide**

It emerges that the old woman has the magical power to offer the knight a choice. He can either accept her the way she is, in which case she will always be faithful and obedient; or else she can make herself young and beautiful, but he must then suffer her infidelity. The knight considers the problem but in the end asks her to make the choice, saying that whatever pleases her best will please him also.

The choice the knight is offered mirrors the anti-female material in the Wife's prologue where every woman was said to have a fault. The misogynist idea that beautiful women must be faithless is one we have heard before: 'And if that she be fair, thou verray knave, / Thou seist that every holour wol hire have' (lines 253–4). It is an **anti-feminist** belief which is now being used to torment a misogynist knight. But he has now learned something from the Loathly Lady. He learned that the answer to the riddle was 'maistrie' but now he really learns what this means and hands over the choice to the woman.

delit desire
fulfille youre worldly appetit satisfy your sexual urge
tweye two
And take youre ... cause of me and take your chances with the male visitors who will turn up at your house because of me
may wel be very likely
wheither that yow liketh whichever one you please
avyseth him and sore siketh reflects and sighs deeply
I do no fors I don't care
For as yow ... suffiseth me as long as you are happy, it is enough for me

LINES 1236–64   The old woman becomes a young, beautiful and faithful wife and they live happily ever after

Having had the mastery handed over to her, the old woman becomes everything the knight would want – beautiful, young, faithful and obedient to him in all things. The knight takes her in his arms and they live 'in perfect joy' ever afterwards. 'And so,' concludes the Wife of Bath, 'may God send us meek, young husbands who are lively in bed, and may we always outlive them. And let Jesus shorten the lives of husbands who don't obey their wives and send a plague on the miserly ones.'

The knight is no longer the misogynist monster he was at the beginning of the tale. He has been transformed into a human being. The Loathly Lady is now able to transform herself too. His gift of sovereignty is returned in her obedience and no-one really has the upper hand any more. But the Wife does not end there. The romance ending gives way to comedy and the battle of the sexes once more (see Textual Analysis – Text 3).

as me lest as I please

sterven wood die insane

emperice empress

my lyf and deth existence

Cast up the curtin lift up the curtain. The bed is a four-poster with hangings all around

hente took

a-rewe in succession

fressh abedde full of sexual vigour

t'overbide to outlive

nigardes of dispence misers

verray pestilence a veritable plague

PART THREE

CRITICAL APPROACHES

CHARACTERISATION OF THE WIFE OF BATH

There is nothing shy or retiring about the character of the Wife of Bath. She is large and noisy, partly due to her deafness, and irrepressibly bossy. In fact, she alone of all the pilgrims manages to force her way into other people's tales (the Clerk and the Merchant both refer to her in the course of their own stories). This is not surprising, as the Wife always seems to have had great power over men. Men and sex are, in fact, two of her main interests and she is not at all shy when it comes to talking about them. She is also not afraid to show us her devious nature. She is a clever woman whose tricks and schemes have got her through five marriages already and she is ready for the sixth husband whenever he happens to come along.

This cleverness together with her warmth and enthusiasm mean that the Wife is forgiven for her more outrageous tricks. She led her old husbands a merry dance and yet she 'tikled' (line 395) their hearts. Nor was her own heart made of stone. Her fourth husband's infidelity rouses her to fury and we see a vulnerable side to her. She had relied on her youth and her beauty to get her through life but now both of these are gone. She is not, however, bitter. Her regrets are dismissed with a cheery 'Lat go, farewel' (line 476) and she looks to the future with optimism.

Some critics have felt that Chaucer's description of the Wife of Bath is so detailed and lifelike that he must have had a real-life model for her. Attempts have been made to identify her with various female cloth-makers in Bath and with an Irish woman tried for witchcraft. But none of these suggestions are likely to be true. Chaucer did have sources for the Wife's character but they were not real people. Instead he was influenced by a lot of literary sources such as works on astrology and also the anti-women literature written in the Middle Ages.

ASTROLOGY AND PHYSIOGNOMY

The Wife of Bath is very fond of defining her own character for us. She has it all worked out according to the influences of astrology and physiognomy (telling someone's character by how they look). She is, she tells us, a Taurean and therefore born under the influence of the planet Venus. But the planet Mars was also in the picture at the time of her birth. She therefore claims to be influenced by both the love goddess Venus and the warrior god Mars. Between them they indicate the dominant traits of the Wife's personality: 'Venus me yaf my lust, my likerousnesse, / And Mars yaf me my sturdy hardinesse.' (lines 611–12) Venus has made her fond of love and Mars has given her great strength of character. Basically, the Wife likes sex and is bold enough to do something about it.

People in the Middle Ages also felt that a person's appearance was influenced by their birth sign. Taureans were supposed to be large with rosy faces. And they were also supposed to like dressing up and going out and about so that they could be admired. The Wife fits this description exactly with what the *General Prologue* calls her 'hipes large', and her desire to go 'for to se, and eek for to be seye' (line 552) wearing her 'gaye scarlet gites' (line 559).

Alison also thinks that there is a lot which can be derived about her personality from her appearance and uses the art of physiognomy to tell us more about herself. She has a birthmark which she is fond of telling us about, down in a 'privee place' (line 620). Physiognomists believed that birthmarks were caused by the position of the stars at the moment of birth and the Wife's seems to prove that she has a voracious sexual nature. She is also gap-toothed which was believed to indicate a lecherous and bold personality. The Wife is thrilled to point this out, 'that bicam me weel' (line 603) she declares gleefully.

Therefore, in some ways, the Wife is a textbook Taurean. She has all the qualities we would expect to find if we looked up a medieval astrological handbook and Chaucer no doubt had one to hand when he created her. But she is also more than a bundle of rules about planetary influence. Nothing in the stars could prepare us for her love for her fifth husband, for example. Her Taurean with Mars horoscope prepares us for a bull in a brothel but there is more to the Wife than this. She is capable of sensitivity and of being hurt in love. Chaucer appears to be showing us that people cannot be reduced to rules. In the end we can see that astrology is important to the Wife, not because it forms her character but because she can say that it does while she has her fun. She can run around with men and lead them a merry dance and put the whole thing down to the influence of her gap-teeth and the fact that she was born on a certain day. Chaucer is therefore allowing the Wife to play a game with the textbooks.

THE FEMALE STEREOTYPE

Chaucer also exploits the notion of the female stereotype in his creation of the Wife of Bath. The misogynists' idea of women as a source of all trouble and evil is an important one (see Literary Background, on The Anti-Feminist Tradition). First of all, many of the things that medieval anti-feminists said about women are true of our Alison. She certainly is a troublemaker and does make her husbands suffer. She is bossy and lustful, has a quick temper and is prone to telling lies on occasion. However, these are not the actions of a stupid woman who cannot help herself. These are the actions of a woman who is fully aware of what the stereotypes about women are and who is willing to use them to her own advantage. She knows, for example, that women are supposed to be irrational, stubborn and emotional while men are supposed to be calm, rational and reasonable. All right then, says Alison to her husband:

> Oon of us two moste bowen, douteless;
>
> And sith a man is moore resonable
>
> Than womman is, ye moste been suffrable. (lines 440–2)

She makes them give in to her by saying that their 'superior' male nature should make them give up the fight more easily. She therefore wins by exploiting all the stereotypes about women.

Without the stereotypes there would be no character of the Wife of Bath. But she is not herself a stereotype. Instead, Chaucer exploits all the traditional things that men wrote about women and creates a woman who is bigger than all of them. She is a very complex character, new and original but created out of traditions which are very ancient.

THEMES

The Wife's natural, and sometimes rambling, talking style means that she does not remain on one topic for very long. However, three closely related themes emerge from her prologue and tale: sexuality, marriage and dominance.

SEXUALITY

The medieval Church did not approve of sex. Some theologians even went so far as to say that Adam and Eve would never have had sex in Paradise and only did so after they had surrendered themselves to the Devil. This view was felt to be too harsh by many but even the most liberal thinkers felt that sex should exist only within marriage and only for the purposes of having children. Women, however, were regarded as dangerously sexual creatures. Medieval science viewed them as having cold bodies which constantly desired contact with the heat of the male. Therefore, it was seen as a woman's nature to crave sex insatiably.

The Wife of Bath is not offended by this view of women. Rather, she glories in it. She will not apologise and try to suppress what is regarded as 'natural'. Instead she takes this word as her defence. The text is full of references to her sexual nature. She declares that in all her life she has never withheld her 'chambre of Venus from a good felawe' (line 618) and this together with her 'bele chose' (line 447) and her less politely named 'queynte' (line 444) is the part of her anatomy we become best acquainted with in the course of the text. The vagina, normally not mentioned or mentioned only to be condemned by medieval authors, is spoken of with enthusiasm by the Wife. Female sexuality is not presented as sinful. The only sexual sin in the text is the rape committed by the knight in the tale. This all-consuming 'desire' for sex is therefore found not in a woman, as the medieval texts suggested, but in a man.

DOMINANCE

Much of the sex in the text, however, has little to do with desire and a lot to do with power. The rape, for example, shows the knight exercising power over the woman. And the task the women of the court set the rapist is an attempt to regain that power. He must find out what it is that women most desire and the answer is revealed to be dominance over men. This, however, is not just the theme of the tale. It is a theme which is crucial to the Wife's prologue. Alison tells how she dominated her first three husbands, struggled to dominate her fourth, and finally succeeded in dominating her fifth. But the theme extends beyond her married life. In the real world of the fourteenth century, very few women would have dominated men. The rules of society placed them in a position where they had to obey. The Wife challenges all such authority. She dominates the men in her life and also tries to dominate male texts, taking them and twisting them for her own purposes.

MARRIAGE

Domination and marriage are, therefore, closely linked. Marriage and sexuality are also interrelated themes. As said earlier, the medieval Church was willing to permit sex within marriage, but it should be pointed out that it would have preferred people not to marry at all. There was a hierarchy which placed virgins at the top, then widows who did not remarry, and then married people at the bottom. It was felt that God must love virgins most and that married people came a very poor third in his affections. The Wife spends the first section of her prologue defending the married state and the other two thirds describing it. She then tells a tale which centres around a marriage.

NARRATIVE TECHNIQUES

We are not sure who or what would have come before *The Wife of Bath's Prologue and Tale* in Chaucer's original plan (see Note on the Text) but the text as it stands suits the Wife's style very much. She bursts onto the scene with no introduction and no invitation and yet it is immediately clear who is speaking: our resident expert on marriage and one of the most natural born talkers in the history of literature.

There is no reason, of course, why this woman should suddenly be speaking of the 'wo that is in mariage' (line 3). After all, as far as we can see, no-one has invited her to do so. But the startled reader feels as though they have been caught napping and must hurry to catch up with the Wife's train of thought. In fact, it is a little bit like trying to catch an express train as she hurtles from one topic to the next. She occasionally loses us, and herself, stopping in the middle of her prologue to declare: 'But now, sire, lat me se, what shal I seyn? / A ha! by God, I have my tale ageyn' (lines 585–6).

The style Chaucer gives her is that of a natural talker, rushing from one topic to the next and giving the impression that, if we do not understand what is going on, then we are the ones at fault. But this is not just idle chit chat, even if it often seems that way. The Wife has an agenda. Her prologue is linked to the tradition of medieval debate (see Literary Background) and she has an argument to win. Chaucer gives the Wife a number of techniques which help her to fight against all the men who have ever written bad things about women. However, he does not let her become too clever. Some of her arguments are convincing but some are not. And often we are meant to see through some of what she says once we have time to think about it. She uses many techniques but the most common are:

Fast talking
Reversing the argument
Literal approach
Undermining the enemy

FAST TALKING

The first of the Wife's debating techniques is her great capacity for talking and ability to race from one topic to the next. This is evident right from the beginning of her prologue. She says that she will speak of the woe in marriage, a proper enough topic for the Middle Ages, but we swiftly move from the word 'woe' to the word 'marriage'. Then, she asks, can she strictly say 'marriage' when she has been married so many times? After all, how many husbands can a woman have had in her life? And should she have ever married in the first place? Does God really want people to be virgins instead? Is that because all sex is wrong? And lo and behold, we suddenly find that we are talking about sex, a subject which interested the Wife of Bath much more all along. However, the audience does not have time to wonder about how they got here.

The same dazzlingly fast style of talking is seen when the Wife is discussing virginity. On first impression she seems to make some convincing points. Her observation that the world needs sex to produce children to produce the next batch of virgins (lines 69–72) leaves the reader marvelling at the logic of it all. Meanwhile, the Wife has already moved on to the topic of St Paul's virginity. However, if we stop for a moment we may remember that the Wife does not in fact ever mention having any children of her own. Indeed, her later accounts of sex with her husbands focus entirely on power and pleasure. Nowhere does she mention any desire to continue the species or produce a little virgin for the greater glory of God. But this is unlikely to occur to the reader at the time. The Wife is so full of enthusiasm, so lively and so quick to move on to her next point that she generally goes unchallenged, at least at first.

REVERSING THE ARGUMENT

The Wife also adopts the tricks of debate which men normally use against women. One of these is the habit of only presenting one side of an argument, or only part of a quotation from the Bible – the part that suits you. For example, preachers in the Middle Ages were very fond of telling women that they must obey their husbands. This, they said, was the way God wanted the world to be and St Paul says so in the Bible. St Paul does say that a woman must behave well towards her husband but he also says that a husband must behave well towards his wife too. Medieval preachers tended to ignore this side of the equation but the Wife of Bath does not. She takes revenge on all those who used the Bible to tell women what to do and starts shouting about a husband's duty. A wife has certain rights, she declares, because St Paul said so! For the first time the one-sided argument is working in women's favour. We might not take it seriously but we are made to see how unfair or even ridiculous it is to quote only the part of the Bible which suits us.

LITERAL APPROACH

Another thing the Wife does is challenge the male habit of 'glosing' or interpreting the Bible. She sees that men have a habit of twisting an interpretation to suit themselves and so she goes back to the Bible and presents it literally. For example, medieval scholars often interpreted marriages in the Bible not as the union of a man and a woman but as a **metaphor** for the union of Christ and the Church. The Wife will not stand for this and instead insists on taking it all literally, particularly the bits in the Old Testament about the patriarchs having many marriages. For every quote from the Bible approved of by the celibate Church, the Wife will find another one which suits her own purposes:

> Men may devine and glosen, up and doun,
> But wel I woot, expres, withoute lie,

God bad us for to wexe and multiplie;

That gentil text kan I wel understonde. (lines 26–9)

Before we congratulate her for championing the truth, however, there is one thing to remember. The Wife herself is an expert glossator and as capable of twisting scripture for her own purposes as any man.

UNDERMINING THE ENEMY

The Wife is fully aware of all the terrible things which men have written about women. Women in the Middle Ages would have heard these things so often that they would have been able to quote examples very easily. Alison could certainly do so. In fact, this is what she does at various parts of her prologue. She uses the work of Jerome frequently, including this passage from the *Epistle Against Jovinian*:

> A continual dripping on a wintry day forces a man out of doors, and so will an
> argumentative woman drive a man from his own house. She floods his house with
> constant nagging and daily chatter, and ousts him from his own home, that is the
> Church. (*Epistle Against Jovinian*, I, 28).

However, this is not quoted respectfully as it is elsewhere in medieval literature. Instead the Wife uses it for her own purposes. She presents it as the kind of abuse which women always have to put up with from their husbands:

> Thow seist that dropping houses, and eek smoke,
> And chiding wives maken men to flee
> Out of hir owene hous; a, *benedicitee*!
> What eyleth swich an old man for to chide? (lines 278–81)

The meaning is no longer cloaked in references to man's relationship with the Church. It is now seen clearly for what it was all along, a spiteful piece of misogyny. And it no longer sounds like the grand musings of a saint and right-hand-man to the pope. Jerome has been reduced to a nagging old man whose hatred of women has been exposed. But again, the matter is not so simple. We should remember that these are not the words of the old husbands. These are the words of a woman quoting a man in order to control other men. It is a complicated device.

AMBIGUITY AND IRONY

In the end, the narrative is constructed in such a way that we do not know who we are supposed to support, or even if we are supposed to support anybody. The Wife is shown to be a likeable character with many persuasive arguments but her prologue is full of contradictions. For every argument which shows the Wife in a good light there is another one which undermines her. This ambiguity is true not just of the Wife's arguments but also of individual words and phrases within the text.

One example of this is the Wife's description of her attitude towards men. She declares that she always followed her 'appetit':

> Al were he short, or long, or blak, or whit;
>
> I took no kep, so that he liked me,
>
> How poore he was, ne eek of what degree. (lines 624–6)

The phrase 'so that he liked me' is dangerously ambiguous. It could mean either 'providing I liked him' or 'providing he liked me'. The difference in words is small but the difference in meaning is vast. The first interpretation makes her an honest, if liberal, lover; the second makes her a crazed nymphomaniac who lives up to all the worst stereotypes about women. However, it is a device which Chaucer uses often. By making some of his points ambiguous he leaves us in doubt so that we cannot entirely support or entirely condemn the Wife of Bath.

LANGUAGE AND STYLE

The Wife's style is vivid and distinctive and very much what we might have expected from the gap-toothed, red-stocking-wearing Wife of the *General Prologue*. Hers is not the language of a grand lady. It is homely and colloquial, full of proverbs and expressions which would have been used in familiar talk. If something is of no use to the Wife it is 'nat worth a leek' (line 572). If she is happy then she is as jolly as a magpie (line 456). And it is these everyday items which make up her world. The Wife knows long words but she tends not to use them herself. Mostly, she holds them in reserve until she is repeating what men say or arguing with them on their own terms. Then we will hear about 'apparaille' (line 343) and 'purgacioun of urine' (lines 121–2) otherwise she is more likely to talk of 'thrifty clooth'(line 238) and 'pisse' (line 729).

There is also something very personal about the Wife's style. This is not surprising given that she is willing to tell us about the intimate goings-on in her bedroom. But the personal style extends beyond her sex life and into all areas of her prologue. She does not talk, for instance, about figures from the Bible in hushed tones of respect. Instead, she speaks as though she knows them. St Paul's letter to the Corinthians sounds like the advice of an old friend:

> Right thus the Apostel tolde it unto me;
> And bad oure housbondes for to love us weel.
> Al this sentence me liketh every deel. (lines 160–2)

And the Biblical command that a man should take a wife sounds, the way the Wife tells it, like a direct instruction from God to her own husband: 'Eek wel I woot, he sayde myn housbonde / Sholde lete fader and mooder, and take to me.' (lines 30–1) At this rate, the reader dare not ask how she knows that Christ was 'shapen as a man' (line 139).

Often, when a character links themselves closely to God or the Bible, they make themselves sound holy too. But the effect is the opposite with the Wife. She does not sound like a saint. Instead the saints sound like ordinary people. 'God' crops up in every other sentence and becomes very familiar in the process. He is in there with the berries (line 659) and the bacon (line 418) and the dishes made of 'tree' (line 101). And if the Wife brings God into her workaday world then no one else is likely to escape the levelling process. Saint Jerome becomes 'a clerk at Rome' (line 673) and King Solomon becomes a fourteenth-century 'sir' (line 35). Apostles, ancient poets and Biblical heroes all share the stage with 'Wilkin, oure sheep' (line 432). They are, of course, not all equal in the Wife's affections – she would seem infinitely to prefer the sheep.

IMAGERY AND SYMBOLISM

ANIMALS

Wilkin is not the only animal to grace *The Wife of Bath's Prologue and Tale*, though he is the only sheep. There are also, in rough order of appearance, a chough, spaniel, goose, ox, ass, hound, gnat, cat, hawk, magpie, nightingale, colt, two mice, two horses, three lions, a lioness, a bittern and various assorted insects. This is not wholly unexpected, given the Wife's homely style of talking, as anyone who talks about leeks and bacon is likely to get round to the farmyard world of cats, mice, geese and oxen eventually. But there are rather too many animals here and some are very exotic.

The animal imagery is in fact used almost entirely to refer to women. The Wife says of herself that she was as 'joly' as a magpie (line 456) but could bite like a horse when she did not get her way (line 386) and she describes her taste for younger men as her 'colte's tooth' (line 602). Not all these references, however, are of the Wife's choosing. She says that her husband accused her of being like a cat whose skin should be singed to make it stay at home. Otherwise,

> ... if the cattes skin be slik and gay
> She wol nat dwelle in house half a day,
> But forth she wole, er any day be dawed,
> To shewe hir skin, and goon a-caterwawed. (lines 351–4)

Women and animals share a very close existence in this text which is not surprising when we consider how the Middle Ages felt about both of them. When God created the world he created man in his own image. Women came after men in the hierarchy and then came the animals. This put women close to the animals on the scale and they were often compared with them, usually in an unflattering way. Animals traditionally symbolise lack of reason and it is interesting that men are only compared to animals in this text when they are out of control and 'dronken as a mous' (line 246) or mad as a lion (line 794).

The Wife is happy to declare herself a 'leonesse' (line 637). But this in fact links her closely to her old archenemy, St Jerome. St Jerome was frequently painted in the Middle Ages with a tame lion lying at his feet. The power of his goodness was allegedly enough to tame the savage beast. But the Wife asks a very significant question in the course of her prologue: 'Who peyntede the leon, tel me who?' (line 692). This is a reference to an old story about a lion who sees a man painting a picture of a lion being killed by a man. It is an interesting picture, says the lion, but if he had painted it the roles would have been reversed. Chaucer means us to see that this was the position of women in the Middle Ages: they often appeared in literature but it was always in the works of men where they could be condemned and presented as the inferior sex. In *The Wife of Bath's Prologue and Tale* the lion, or lioness, is at last getting the chance to paint the picture. The Wife is turning all the material round and showing us matters from the female point of view. The lion will no longer lie down with St Jerome, it will instead be a proper fierce lion and challenge his position of authority.

And the Wife is very happy with the animal imagery applied to her. St Jerome and the medieval Church wanted people to turn away from the flesh and think only of the spirit. But the Wife reminds everyone that people are not only 'spirit', that they have good healthy animal bodies too. The purpose of much of the animal imagery here is not to dehumanise people but to challenge the authority which demanded that they be more than human.

TRADE AND COMMERCE

Another kind of imagery frequently used by Chaucer here comes from the world of medieval trade. It has been said that in the Middle Ages marriages were often arranged for economic and political reasons and that love was frequently not the primary reason for a match. And indeed, the Wife of Bath refers repeatedly to relationships in terms of trade and property. Courtship, for example, is described in terms of negotiating at market:

> Greet prees at market maketh deere ware,
> And to greet cheep is holde at litel prys:
> This knoweth every womman that is wys. (lines 521–3)

Anyone interested in attracting a lover should make sure that they seem desirable and hard to get, not something which could be picked up easily, she says.

In the Wife's hands, the old cliché of the 'flower of youth' becomes baking flour. She does not think of her lost youth as a faded rose, she looks upon it like a medieval miller who has sold his good flour and now must sell the bran (lines 477–8). This has led some critics to view the Wife as mercenary. And it is possible that Chaucer is using this imagery to show

how dehumanising the medieval marriage system was. But we should also remember that the Wife is instantly willing to give up all her wealth when she marries Jankyn. It is more likely that the traditional image of woman as 'property' in sexual trade is yet one more stereotype which is being mocked. She might declare that 'all is for to selle' (line 414) but, when the seller is also the thing being sold, then the terms no longer apply and the old barriers break down once again.

PART FOUR

Textual analysis

TEXT 1   (LINES 115–46)

Telle me also, to what conclusion
Were membres maad of generacioun,
And of so parfit wys a wight ywroght?
Trusteth right wel, they were nat maad for noght.
Glose whoso wole, and seye bothe up and doun,
That they were maked for purgacioun
Of urine, and oure bothe thinges smale
Were eek to knowe a femele from a male,
And for noon oother cause, – say ye no?
The experience woot wel it is noght so.
So that the clerkes be nat with me wrothe,
I sey this, that they maked ben for bothe,
This is to seye, for office, and for ese
Of engendrure, ther we nat God displese.
Why sholde men elles in hir bookes sette
That man shal yelde to his wyf hire dette?
Now wherwith sholde he make his paiement,
If he ne used his sely instrument?
Thanne were they maad upon a creature
To purge urine, and eek for engendrure.

But I seye noght that every wight is holde,
That hath swich harneys as I to yow tolde,
To goon and usen hem in engendrure.
Thanne sholde men take of chastitee no cure.
Crist was a maide, and shapen as a man,
And many a seint, sith that the world bigan;
Yet lived they evere in parfit chastitee.
I nil envye no virginitee.
Lat hem be breed of pured whete-seed,
And lat us wives hoten barly-breed;
And yet with barly-breed, Mark telle kan,
Oure Lord Jhesu refresshed many a man.

In the very first line of the prologue, the Wife declares that she will reject authority but she cannot, in fact, stay away from the learned authors of the past and argues against them at every opportunity. Her adversary as this passage opens is, once again, St Jerome and it is fair to say that at this point he is definitely losing. In her characteristic way of getting to the nub of the issue, the Wife demands to know why people were given sexual organs if they were not intended to have sex:

> Telle me also, to what conclusion
> Were membres maad of generacion,
> And of so parfit wys a wight ywroght? (lines 115–7)

Jerome and other learned authors would normally have written in Latin and the Wife begins her question, perhaps a little sarcastically, using grand Latinate words: 'conclusion', 'generacion' and even 'membres'. However, this does not last for long and the whole sentence is comically undercut by the reference to a man's 'wight' or 'thing' in the third line. The Wife will always call a spade a spade or a thing a thing even if the philosophers are too squeamish to do so themselves.

She knows all too well that men will rush to 'glose' (line 119) or twist any truth which they do not like and Jerome is certainly uncomfortable on this subject. He did not want to admit that these organs were intended for any sexual purpose but his suggestion that they were designed only for urinating and so that a male could be differentiated from a female is very weak. The Wife's forthright approach to the subject leaves Jerome looking foolish as she quotes the Bible against him and demands to know how else a man 'shal yelde to his wyf hire dette'? (line 130). It is a great moment. A woman from Bath has taken on one of the great theologians of the Middle Ages, a saint no less, and shown him to be a prudish killjoy with no grip on reality. In fact, she may even have done worse. As he is the only male in the passage, her offhand references to 'thinges smale' (line 121) and 'sely instrument' (line 132) seem dangerously personal. But the Wife's chattering speed means that Chaucer whisks us away before the matter can be considered any further.

The Wife is now generously declaring that not everyone is required by God to use their 'harneys' (line 136). Although she is quite sure that all men from Christ downwards had such 'tackle' (an even more risqué remark than her previous sideswipe at Jerome), she is certain that not every man is obliged to go and use it 'in engendrure' (line 137). This is an amazing reversal of the customary arguments. The Wife herself had begun with the usual question, 'Is everyone required to be a virgin?' Suddenly, the rug has been pulled from under the feet of the learned authorities and ourselves. The old assumptions have been swept away and we find ourselves in a wonderland where the Wife of Bath is telling us that, in spite of all the evidence to the contrary, it is quite all right to be a virgin. She also bolsters up the threatened status of virginity by reassuring us that 'Crist was a maide' (line 139) and some of the saints too. In the light of this, her declaration that she 'nil envye no virginitee' (line 142) seems like an act of great generosity. Logic has disappeared somewhere but we are being carried along by this impressive performance.

By the time the Wife reaches Jerome's famous comparison of married people with barley bread she has the audience eating out of her hand. Christ, Jerome, virgins and saints everywhere are dismissed as 'them' while we bask in the accolade of 'us wives' (line 144). And what she is offering us sounds so much more attractive. Virgins, according to Jerome, are like pure wheaten bread, while the impure are like barley, but the Wife is happy with this comparison: 'Lat hem be breed of pured whete-seed, / And lat us wives hoten barly-breed' (lines 143–4)

In the Wife's hands there is something cold and hard about virginity. The word which sticks in the mind is 'seed' which is not nearly so appealing as the barley bread, especially as it is 'hoten' barley bread. 'Hoten' simply means 'called' but the word 'hot' is obviously not far from the reader's mind. Chaucer could have used the far more common 'cleped' as he does for 'called' three lines later, but he wanted to conjure up a picture of freshly baked bread, warm from the oven as opposed to the cold, hard 'seed' of virginity.

The Wife declares that she is happy to be 'barley-breed' and the audience are unlikely to blame her. She even has another Biblical quotation to strengthen her argument and refers to the miracle of the loaves and fishes which 'Mark telle kan' (line 145). However, a medieval audience would have known that it is not St Mark who mentions barley loaves, it is the gospel of St John. The Wife has made a mistake. It is, of course, only a little mistake but we may begin to wonder what else she has been mistaken about.

And what about St Jerome's comparison, has she got that right?

Jerome did say that virgins were like wheaten bread and that non-virgins
were like barley bread, but the Wife has missed off the end of what he had
to say. In fact, he said that eating barley was only fractionally better than
eating cow dung. The Wife has therefore managed happily to equate
herself with a pile of manure. This is enough to bring the audience round
and make them see that the Wife is not to be trusted in everything. And
yet her points were good ones while they lasted. The Wife, in the
meantime, has already moved on and is calling for her husband to 'pay his
debt' at least twice a day.

TEXT 2   (LINES 371–402)

> Thou liknest eek wommenes love to helle,
> To bareyne lond, ther water may nat dwelle.
> Thou liknest it also to wilde fyr;
> The moore it brenneth, the moore it hath desir
> To consume every thing that brent wole be.
> Thou seyest, right as wormes shende a tree,
> Right so a wyf destroyeth hire housbonde;
> This knowe they that been to wives bonde.'
>   Lordinges, right thus, as ye have understonde,
> Baar I stifly mine olde housbondes on honde
> That thus they seyden in hir dronkenesse;
> And al was fals, but that I took witnesse
> On Janekin, and on my nece also.
> O Lord! the peyne I dide hem and the wo,
> Ful giltelees, by Goddes sweete pine!
> For as an hors I koude bite and whine.
> I koude pleyne, and yit was in the gilt,
> Or elles often time hadde I been spilt.
> Whoso that first to mille comth, first grint;
> I pleyned first, so was oure werre ystint.
> They were ful glade to excuse hem blive
> Of thing of which they never agilte hir live.
> Of wenches wolde I beren hem on honde,
> Whan that for sik unnethes mighte they stonde.
>   Yet tikled I his herte, for that he

> Wende that I hadde of him so greet chiertee.
>
> I swoor that al my walkinge out by nighte
>
> Was for t'espie wenches that he dighte;
>
> Under that colour hadde I many a mirthe.
>
> For al swich wit is yeven us in oure birthe;
>
> Deceite, weping, spinning God hath yive
>
> To womman kindely, whil that they may live.

This passage comes from the second section of the Wife's prologue where she is giving an account of her life with her first three husbands. It is particularly interesting for the imagery which it uses.

The Wife has just finished saying that her husbands would like her to be singed like a cat to make her stay at home. Now, however, women have been pushed even further down the evolutionary scale and are compared to 'wormes' (line 376) which strip a tree bare. It is a grotesque comparison but to the medieval mind it would have been even worse than it first appears. 'Worme' can also mean 'serpent' in medieval English and the subtle combination of 'worme', 'tree' and a woman who 'destroyeth hire housbonde' (line 377) brings us to the old favourite of anti-feminists everywhere – Eve. Eve's shadow looms over this passage as it does over much of the prologue. Because of Eve women were destined to live in sorrow and sin: 'Deceite, weping, spinning God hath yive / To wommen kindely, whil that they may live.' (lines 401–2) Deceit, sorrow and hard labour are Eve's legacy to women according to the medieval authorities. But this definition of a woman, like so many stereotypes, is overturned by the Wife of Bath in the course of her prologue. In place of Eve sitting humbly spinning as punishment for her sin, we have the Wife's profitable cloth-making business. In the *General Prologue* we hear that, 'Of clooth-making she hadde swich an haunt, / She passed hem of Ypres and of Gaunt' (lines 449–50).

In fact, the cloth-makers of the West Country (including Bath) were so bad that English merchants abroad sometimes had to run for their lives and we should not take Chaucer's praise too seriously. But the Wife's 'spinning' is a far cry from the pitiful sight of Eve cast out of Paradise. If the Wife is a 'daughter of Eve' she is doing very well for herself.

As for the 'weping' in the equation, the Wife seems to do very little of this. All the sorrow seems to belong to her husbands. And most of this is caused by her 'deceit'. In fact, the whole passage is based on deceit. The old husbands neither invented the insults at the beginning nor chased the wenches (line 398) at the end. It is all a fantasy composed by the Wife to conceal her own misdemeanours. And yet, the Wife did not actually invent all the terrible insults either. These were already the stock-in-trade of the anti-women writers and were used to condemn women everywhere. It is not surprising therefore that the Wife should choose to fight back.

And the language of this passage suggests that men and women are very much engaged in a battle of the sexes. The Wife is always keen to point out that her horoscope is influenced by Mars, the god of war and it is this word, 'werre' (line 390), which describes her relationship with the old husbands. Women are also compared to 'wilde fyr' (line 373), a weapon used in naval warfare.

The image of woman as fire first appears early in the prologue, during the discussion of virginity. There it is stated that a woman coming into contact with a man is like bringing 'fyr and tow t'assemble' (line 89), a perilous business, and one which St Paul advises against if possible. In fact, the idea of woman as fire is found in all the **anti-feminist writings**. In his medieval encyclopedia, the *Etymologiae*, Isidore of Seville claims that the name 'female' comes from the Greek word for fire ('fos'):

> Some think she is called 'female' from the Greek 'fos' meaning 'burning force' because of the intensity of her desire. For females are more lustful than males in both humans and animals. (*Etymologiae*, XI, ii, 23)

And St Jerome describes a woman's love in much the same way:

> The love of any woman, not just the whore or the adulteress, is always insatiable. If you attempt to put it out it will only burst into flame again. If you feed the fire it will be soon in need once more. (*Epistle Against Jovinian*, I, 28)

Thus, there were two things which were associated with fire in the Middle Ages – women and hell. Women are compared to fire throughout the prologue and tale, from the singed cat to the wife of Midas 'a-fire' (line 971) with a secret. The imagery is at its anti-women best in this passage where hell, fire, and women all come together in the one **simile**:

> Thou liknest eek wommenes love to helle,
> To bareyne lond, ther water may nat dwelle.
> Thou liknest it also to wilde fyr;
> The moore it brenneth, the moore it hath desir
> To consume every thing that brent wole be. (lines 371–5)

But it is an image which is going to be changed in the course of the text. It is an anti-female image here but in the tale it later becomes a symbol of true nobility and female superiority. When the Loathly Lady gives her lecture on 'gentillesse' she reclaims the image of the fire which will not go out from the anti-feminist writers:

> Taak fyr, and ber it in the derkeste hous
> Bitwix this and the mount of Kaukasous,
> And lat men shette the dores and go thenne;
> Yet wole the fyr as faire lie and brenne. (lines 1139–42)

In the hands of a female narrator the fire becomes a positive symbol. It just depends, as Chaucer has shown us throughout, on the viewpoint of the speaker.

TEXT 3   (LINES 1228–64)

> This knight aviseth him and sore siketh,
> But atte laste he seyde in this manere:
> 'My lady and my love, and wyf so deere,
> I put me in youre wise governance;
> Cheseth youreself which may be moost plesance
> And moost honour to yow and me also.
> I do no fors the wheither of the two;
> For as yow liketh, it suffiseth me.'
>   'Thanne have I gete of yow maistrie,' quod she,
> 'Sin I may chese and governe as me lest?'
>   'Ye, certes, wyf,' quod he, 'I holde it best.'
>   'Kis me,' quod she, 'we be no lenger wrothe;
> For, by my trouthe, I wol be to yow bothe,
> This is to seyn, ye, bothe fair and good.
> I prey to God that I moote sterven wood,
> But I to yow be also good and trewe
> As evere was wyf, sin that the world was newe.
> And but I be to-morn as fair to seene
> As any lady, emperice, or queene,
> That is bitwixe the est and eke the west,
> Dooth with my lyf and deth right as yow lest.

Cast up the curtin, looke how that it is.'
    And whan the knight saugh verraily al this,
That she so fair was, and so yong therto,
For joye he hente hire in his armes two,
His herte bathed in a bath of blisse.
A thousand time a-rewe he gan hire kisse,
And she obeyed him in every thing
That mighte doon him plesance or liking.
    And thus they live unto hir lives ende
In parfit joye; and Jhesu Crist us sende
Housbondes meeke, yonge, and fressh abedde,
And grace t'overbide hem that we wedde;
And eek I praye Jhesu shorte hir lives
That wol nat be governed by hir wives;
And olde and angry nigardes of dispence,
God sende hem soone verray pestilence!

The Wife of Bath's Tale comes closest to the medieval genre of romance, with elements of fairytale thrown in. Medieval romance was very popular and Chaucer's audience would have known exactly what to expect: a tale of beautiful ladies and noble knights engaged in acts of bravery for honourable causes. However, there is not a single **genre** in *The Wife of Bath's Prologue and Tale* which turns out the way we would expect it to. What starts off looking like a confession turns out to be a boastful account of sin; the sermon form is used not by a celibate priest but by a woman who wants to talk about sex; and the misogynist tales are turned inside out and used by a wife against her husbands. It should not come as a surprise, therefore, that the romance genre is turned on its head in the Wife's tale. Knights are supposed to save fair damsels in distress. Here, the damsel is ugly, the knight is in distress and it is the damsel who must do the saving.

The traditional choice is also turned round. Normally the knight is offered a wife fair by day or fair by night (see Literary Background), giving him the choice of either public or private pleasure. But the decision required here is very different. It is a misogynist choice based on the principle already outlined in the prologue that every woman has faults (lines 248–76). His wife can be either fair and faithless or else foul and faithful. Our knight is not, therefore, choosing his form of pleasure. Rather, he has to decide which way his wife is going to make him miserable. Man has become completely powerless and woman is completely in control. It is no wonder that the knight 'sore siketh' (line 1228). But he is no longer the selfish rapist who turned from his ugly wife in disgust and a fit of temper. The Loathly Lady and her speech on 'gentillesse' have educated him and turned round his ideas about women. This can be seen not only in his decision to give the choice to his wife but also in the words which Chaucer has carefully given him: 'I do no fors the wheither of the two' (line 1234) This means, of course, that he 'does not mind' which one she chooses but the word 'fors' is crucial because the knight's crime had been using this 'force' against women. And the exercise of force or power against women has been the Wife of Bath's theme throughout. The knight's claim to 'do no fors', therefore, has far wider implications than this one decision. He is surrendering the male power which is always used against women. His lesson has been truly learned.

Again, in the sources, the old woman shows herself to her husband as beautiful and then asks him to make his choice. And it is easy to imagine that a knight, confronted by a beautiful woman, might tell her to do exactly what she wants. But our Loathly Lady stays firmly behind the curtain. Our knight has no idea about the pleasures which might be his. In spite of this, he addresses her in the kindest and nicest terms: 'My lady and my love and wyf so deere' (line 1230). He cannot have been swayed by her beauty because he has not seen her. The change in his attitude is entirely the result of his wife's teaching and his new, genuinely noble character.

He has been transformed and offers her the 'maistrie'. In the other romances this breaks the spell but the case here is slightly different. The Loathly Lady is not under some cruel spell. The ability to change has been in her own power all along. 'I wol be to yow ... bothe fair and good' (lines 1240–1), she tells him. The choice of this word 'wol' shows that the power has been in her own hands, the subject of her own 'will' all the time. She is not some poor enchanted woman, she is a symbol of female power and domination. However, she will only transform her character when the knight transforms his. When he stops being the stereotypical man (dominating, cruel, violent), then she abandons the stereotypical choice (that a beautiful woman must be faithless). The stereotypes are therefore swept away as she becomes good and beautiful and they fall into one another's arms.

It is the same process which we see at the end of *The Wife of Bath's Prologue*. When the Wife fell in love with Jankin she wanted to get away from misogynistic ideas about women and love him as herself.

But just as there were still worrying aspects at the end of the prologue, so there are still worrying aspects at the end of the tale. On the surface the knight seems to have given his wife control and she in her turn 'obeyed him in every thing / That mighte doon him plesance or liking' (lines 1255–6). This seems to say that in practice neither one had the 'maistrie' but that they lived instead in a state of mutual love and understanding. But their arrangement can also be seen in more cynical terms. Perhaps it only means that the wife was sexually obliging once she had got her own way. This seems like a very harsh interpretation and could be dismissed if the Wife were not breathing down our necks again. The moment her tale is finished she is calling out for more husbands 'meeke, yonge, and fressh abedde' (line 1259).

We are simply not allowed to see the end of the tale without thinking of its teller. And with this in mind we may begin to see other worrying aspects about the ending. The wife does not simply promise to be good and true, she promises to be as 'good and trewe / As evere was wyf, sin that the world was newe' (lines 1243–4). On the surface it is a lovely thought but after hearing the Wife of Bath's prologue we must be painfully aware of who the first 'wyf' was when the 'world was newe'. It was, of course, Eve who 'al mankinde broght to wrecchednesse' (line 716). Her promise is therefore a chilling one, if we want to read it that way.

Our final image is not of the happy couple. It is of the Wife of Bath calling for fresh victims. She is not defending the harmony which her tale may be suggesting. Instead, she is calling for the 'grace t'overbide hem that we wedde' (line 1260). It is her old appeal for dominance and there is also the familiar curse on old and miserly husbands whom she wants to suffer 'pestilence'. This final rhyme takes us back to the first word of the prologue – 'experience'. Maybe we have only come full circle or maybe we have learned something on the way. Chaucer does not resolve the issue. He leaves us with the images of married bliss, young husbands and the Wife of Bath all swimming together in our heads.

PART FIVE

BACKGROUND

GEOFFREY CHAUCER

Geoffrey Chaucer was born in London in the early 1340s, most probably in 1343, the son, possibly the only son, of John Chaucer and his wife Agnes. The family originated in Ipswich where they had been called de Dynyngton or le Taverner and it seems likely that Geoffrey Chaucer's great-grandfather had been a tavern keeper. Geoffrey's grandfather, Robert de Dynyngton, appears to have worked for a merchant but when the merchant died in a brawl in 1302 Robert inherited some of his property. The family were now far more prosperous and as a result of this change in fortune they also changed their name. They took the name of their dead benefactor: Chaucer.

They settled in London where John Chaucer, Geoffrey's father, became a very prosperous wine merchant. He supplied wine to the king's cellars, supervising imports from France. He was influential and successful and was heavily involved in the business and political affairs of the city. His wealth and connections meant that he could provide his young son with many advantages, beginning with Geoffrey's enrolment as a page in the royal household.

A page was a boy between the ages of ten and seventeen who was an attendant in the house of a noble family. Effectively he was a servant but in this way a boy would learn about polite society and hopefully be accepted by a patron, someone who would take an interest in him and help his career. The young Geoffrey became a page to the Countess of Ulster, the king's daughter-in-law, and eventually served her husband, Prince Lionel.

It was in the service of Prince Lionel that Geoffrey was captured in France. Edward III made an unsuccessful attempt to gain the French throne in 1359 and Geoffrey Chaucer is named among those for whom a ransom was paid. After this, he seems to have entered the direct service of the king though his diplomatic skills seem to have been more in demand than his military expertise. He was sent on diplomatic missions to Spain, France and Italy over the next few years and some of his business appears to have been of a very secret nature.

Chaucer's social standing was also improved by his marriage in 1365 to Philippa Pan (or de Roet), a lady in the household of Queen Philippa, Edward III's wife. Philippa's sister Katherine was the mistress, and eventually the third wife, of John of Gaunt, the rich and powerful son of Edward III. Chaucer's marriage to Philippa therefore connected him more intimately to the rich and powerful circle of John of Gaunt and the royal court. John's son by his first marriage would later become King Henry IV and Chaucer's nephews were therefore half-brothers to the future king.

However, Chaucer's daily life does not seem to have been drastically affected by his family connections. In fact, in 1374 he was appointed to a new position with the customs department in London, a move which took him away from court. He was responsible for checking the quantities of wool, sheepskins and hides being shipped abroad so that the correct export duty could be charged. He was still sent overseas on state business and these trips probably brought him into contact with the works of the great European poets.

In 1389 he was appointed to a new position: clerk of the king's works. Still a civil servant, his new post meant that he was in charge of overseeing the building and repair of the king's properties. He supervised the workmen, paid the wages and saw that the plans were properly implemented. However, paying the wages proved to be more of a problem than it sounds. Chaucer was robbed, certainly once but possibly three times in the space of four days, as he attempted to deliver the money. It may have been a relief, therefore, when he was instructed to give up the post a few months later.

Chaucer now retired from the king's service but he continued to receive annual payments from the court, together with gifts such as a fur-trimmed, scarlet gown from the future Henry IV and an annual tun (252 gallons) of wine from Richard II. An occasional poem on the state of his purse ensured that his pension arrived on time but most of his creative energy was focused on one work, *The Canterbury Tales*. This was the last decade of Chaucer's life. He died on 25 October 1400, *The Canterbury Tales* still unfinished. He was buried in one of the more humble chapels in Westminster Abbey but his body was later moved to the east aisle of the south transept, where he became the first tenant of 'Poets' Corner'.

CHAUCER AND CECILIA CHAUMPAIGNE

One puzzling fact remains about Chaucer's life which is interesting in the context of *The Wife of Bath's Tale*. A legal document dating from 1380 exists which is still not understood. In it, one Cecilia Chaumpaigne releases Geoffrey Chaucer from all actions concerning her *raptus*. This is an ambiguous word. It can mean abduction, either physically or in the sense of seizing guardianship over a minor. But it can also mean rape. The matter is further complicated by the fact that a man named John Grove is also somehow involved. He certainly paid the fine (a sum equivalent to many months' wages for Chaucer) to Cecilia but his connection is not clear. It has been suggested that he was, in fact, the principal in the matter and not Chaucer. It has also been suggested that the charge was false or merely a threat so that a settlement on a lesser charge could be reached. But it is also possible that Chaucer was the main defendant and that the charge was indeed rape.

HIS OTHER WORKS

The earliest work we have by Chaucer is the *Romaunt of the Rose,* a liberal translation of part of a famous French work. It is an exploration of the nature of love including everything from sex and friendship to love for God. Much of it is satirical and women, and those foolish enough to love them, are a favourite target for abuse.

Chaucer's next major work was probably *The Book of the Duchess,* a poem of consolation for John of Gaunt following the death of his first wife, Blanche, in 1368. *The Parlement of Foules* (Fowls)(c.1380) is also probably linked to an historical event. In this poem a Dreamer watches as the birds gather to choose their mates on St Valentine's Day. The complicated nature of love is seen in the eagle who must choose between her three suitors, possibly a reference to the much courted Anne of Bohemia who finally married Richard II on 3 May 1381.

Love becomes even more complicated and far less successful in Chaucer's next poem, the great *Troilus and Criseyde.* Here Chaucer tells us the story of Prince Troilus who loved Criseyde and how she betrayed him before she died. However, in his next poem, Chaucer declares that he will make amends to women. In *The Legend of Good Women* he tells how the

God of Love chastised him for telling the story of Criseyde and for translating his *Romaunt of the Rose* and he promises (we assume not wholly seriously) to tell only good stories about women in future. He worked for a few years on this project but never finished it, turning his attention instead to *The Canterbury Tales* around 1387.

Like *The Legend of Good Women*, *The Canterbury Tales* is a collection of individual stories but the tone and setting are very different. This is not presented as a dream populated by gods and goddesses but is instead a tale of ordinary people set in the real world of the fourteenth century. There is a Knight in the company and some of the group (the Wife of Bath included) do tell stories about knights and ladies but Chaucer is no longer only concerned with the court. Merchants, millers, ploughmen and sailors are all the object of his attention. The issues which had concerned him in his earlier poetry are still found here but given wider application. Almost all medieval society rides up to tell a tale and these are as likely to be humorous and obscene as courtly and tragic.

HISTORICAL BACKGROUND

One day in October 1347, a boat arrived in the port of Messina in Sicily. When the hatches were opened the boat was found to be full of dead and dying men, their bodies swollen and blackened by some terrible disease. The bubonic plague, the Black Death, had arrived in Europe. It spread quickly, carried by black rats who nested on board ships, and was transmitted to humans through flea-bites. By 1349 the disease had taken hold in England and within the year around a third of the population (1.5 million) were dead.

The deaths of so many people inevitably had a powerful effect on medieval life. The traditional picture of the Middle Ages was of the Church and the aristocracy, both small but powerful groups, being supported by the labour of vast numbers of peasants. This system had already begun to break down by the time Chaucer was born but it had not gone completely. The arrival of the plague, or 'the death' as it was known in the Middle Ages, changed this. For the first time, peasant labour was in short supply. Peasants could no longer be expected to remain on the old estates. They moved instead in greater numbers to the cities where the wages were high.

Those in the towns who survived the plague also profited financially. Geoffrey Chaucer's father, for example, lost many of his relatives but inherited a good deal of property.

People were also no longer confined to the social class into which they were born. The fourteenth century saw a lot of social mobility. The de la Pole family, for example, rose from Hull merchants to the earldom of Suffolk in two generations. And Chaucer's own family went from tavern keepers to esquires at court in less than a hundred years. It is not surprising, therefore, that the question of true 'gentility' should have interested Chaucer in *The Wife of Bath's Tale*.

However, all the changes in the social structure worried those who had always had power. Attempts were made to restore wages and conditions to pre-plague levels and it became an offence for men to seek new masters or higher wages. A poll (or head) tax was also introduced which demanded a shilling from every man and woman in the country, no matter how poor they were. The people grew discontented and then rebellious, resulting in the Peasants' Revolt of 1381.

Violence broke out in Essex and spread to Kent. The rebels marched on London, thousands of them pouring into the city at Aldgate, below Chaucer's house. Together with London workers they burned John of Gaunt's palace and stormed the Tower of London. The chancellor and the treasurer were killed as were civil servants, lawyers and wealthy merchants. The violence was eventually brought under control but English society had changed.

The two great powers of the Middle Ages, the monarchy and the church, were also unstable. Richard II, only fourteen years old when he rode out to face the Peasants' Revolt, was deposed by his own noblemen as they struggled for power. He was forced from the throne by his cousin and died in prison in 1400. The Church was no better. The Papacy had moved from Rome to Avignon in the south of France in the early fourteenth century. In 1378, however, there was suddenly a rival pope set up in Rome. Two popes, both claiming the authority of God, competed for the loyalty of the people for nearly forty years. The Church, like the monarchy, was in a state of conflict and confusion.

This then is the background to Chaucer's *Canterbury Tales*. It was a time of great change in which the status of many people was altered. A new class emerged consisting of merchants, physicians, cooks, businessmen and even business women like the Wife of Bath. However, we should not get the impression that there were women like the Wife roaming all over the country. Even in this climate of change the options open to women remained limited. They had effectively two choices – to marry or enter the Church. It has been estimated that around ninety-two per cent of women chose the first option. And although many worked hard in family businesses and some even ran businesses, a woman was always considered to be under the authority of her husband. She was, in many ways, his 'property' to the extent that the rape of a woman was regarded as a property crime. The idea of an independent lifestyle for women was not an option. They were denied access to all positions of public authority and even privately were supposed to be under the control of men whether that was a husband or a father, or in the case of women who became nuns, the male members of the Church. In this context, the Wife of Bath's challenge to 'authority' seems all the more remarkable.

LITERARY BACKGROUND

In medieval literature telling a story which was new or original was not of primary importance. The popular stories of the Middle Ages had often been around for hundreds or even thousands of years and this was not only accepted, it was encouraged. People who had managed to invent a whole new story often pretended that it was really an old tale that they had heard somewhere. But the important thing was not the age of the story but how it was told. Taking a story and making it interesting was the poet's job, regardless of the age of the tale.

THE WIFE OF BATH'S PROLOGUE

The Wife of Bath's Prologue is, first and foremost, a prologue and such a definition would be sufficient for all the other prologues in *The Canterbury Tales*. But this one is slightly different. For a start, it is 856 lines long, more than twice the length of the Wife's tale and about ten times as long as anyone else's prologue. It therefore requires a little more explanation than most.

In some senses it is an autobiography but such a thing would have been too egotistical for the Middle Ages. People at the end of the fourteenth century occasionally wrote about their lifelong relationship with God but no one sat down to write their own life story just for the sake of it. The closest **genre** in existence was the *confessio* (like a confession) where the subject admitted their past sins and submitted to the will of God. The Wife happily, too happily, admits to her sins but she does not show the necessary desire to change her ways. A medieval audience would have recognised this and part of the humour lies in the Wife's 'confession' of a life spent enjoying herself.

Another of the genres parodied by Chaucer in *The Wife of Bath's Prologue* is the debate or sermon. This involved arguing or teaching on various topics, and the participants were always men. The Wife comically becomes one of these learned authorities as the Pardoner begs her to 'teche us yonge men' (line 187). And she is not averse to employing *disputatio* techniques in her arguments with her husbands. She describes her quarrels with them as if she is talking about a debate:

> For, by my trouthe, I quitte hem word for word...
> I ne owe hem nat a word that it nis quit.
> I broghte it so aboute by my wit
> That they moste yeve it up, as for the beste,
> Or elles hadde we nevere been in reste.
> For though he looked as a wood leon,
> Yet sholde he faille of his conclusion (lines 422–30)

But the Wife's opponent in the prologue is not her husband. She is arguing against every man in the Middle Ages who ever said anything bad about women.

THE ANTI-FEMINIST TRADITION

The Wife of Bath's Prologue consists of all the best known arguments against women used by medieval preachers and moralists. This **anti-feminist literature** is the source for almost the whole prologue. The terms anti-feminist and misogynist both simply mean anti-women. And the anti-feminist or anti-female tradition refers to a way of thinking and writing about women which condemns them in all things.

The idea of women as evil and a source of trouble to men began early.
In fact it began in the Old Testament – with the very first woman. Eve ate
the apple she was told not to touch and succeeded in getting herself, Adam
and all their descendants expelled from Paradise. This story was very
important in the Middle Ages and significantly is the very first tale in
Jankyn's Book of Wicked Wives:

> Of Eva first, that for hir wikkednesse
> Was al mankinde broght to wrecchednesse...
> Lo, heere expres of womman may ye finde,
> That womman was the los of al mankinde. (lines 715–20)

Because of the wickedness and stupidity of a woman, so the story goes, the
whole of humanity was thrown into a cold, hard world where they would
suffer and get sick and die: all things which would never have happened had
they stayed in Paradise. All the woes of the world could therefore be
blamed on a woman.

Eve was a hard act to follow but the Middle Ages were never short of
stories about wicked women, as Jankyn's book shows. But the view of
women as full of vices and inferior to men in all things was applied to every
woman, not just to colourful characters from history. Medieval scholars
presented all women as weak and unintelligent and likely to sin, fond of
causing trouble and bound to make any man miserable who was foolish
enough to marry them. Their bodies were regarded on the one hand as
filthy and inferior, and on the other as a terrible temptation to men, put
there by the devil.

JEROME AND THEOPHRASTUS

One of the best known anti-feminist writers of the Middle Ages was St
Jerome (c.342–420). He was a learned and influential man who was
secretary to Pope Damascus and who spent thirty years translating the
Bible out of Hebrew and Greek and into Latin. A large part of his early life
had been spent in the desert, existing under harsh and extreme conditions.
This lifestyle, however, suited his personality. He held extreme views about
everything but was particularly severe about the human body. Jerome
believed that all desires of the body were sinful. The human desire to sleep,
eat, drink and have sex were all evils in his view. He therefore argued that
the first three should be kept to a minimum and the fourth should not be

indulged in at all. This, he felt, would be so much easier if there were no women around to tempt men and so his writings are full of condemnations of the female sex. Chaucer quotes him frequently in the prologue, usually from his long *Epistle Against Jovinian*. Jovinian was a monk who suggested that people did not have to be virgins to be loved by God. Jerome called this idea 'nauseating trash' and his letter in reply was a favourite source of material for anyone who wanted to condemn women in the Middle Ages.

We know about Theophrastus because Jerome quotes him in his letter. He was allegedly the author of a misogynist work called *The Golden Book on Marriage*. Here is a sample of what he has to say:

> Married women want many things, costly dresses, gold, jewels, expensive items, maidservants, all kinds of furniture, litters and gilded coaches. Then come prattling complaints all the night: that one lady goes out better dressed than she; that another is looked up to by all. 'I am a poor despised nobody at women's gatherings.' 'Why did you ogle that creature next door?' 'Why were you talking to the maid?' 'What did you bring from the market?' we are not allowed to have a single friend or companion; her husband's friendship going elsewhere would entail his hate for her, she suspects.
> There may be in some neighbouring city the wisest of teachers; but if we have a wife we can neither leave her behind, nor take the burden with us.

These lines are in fact used by Chaucer in *The Wife of Bath's Prologue*. But they are not quoted seriously. Instead, Chaucer takes this anti-female speech and gives it to the Wife of Bath:

> Sire olde kaynard, is this thyn array?
> Why is my neighebores wyf so gay?
> She is honoured over al ther she gooth;
> I sitte at hoom, I have no thrifty clooth.
> What dostow at my neighebores hous?
> Is she so fair? artow so amorous?
> What rowne ye with oure maide? *Benedictee!*
> Sire olde lecchour, lat thy japes be. (lines 235–42)

This is no longer a solemn piece of anti-feminist thought. Chaucer has taken the genre and turned it inside out. For a start, the words sound very different when they are coming from a woman and are being used to chastise men.

Therefore, Chaucer relies very heavily on the anti-feminist tradition. He takes lots of pieces from the works of Jerome, Theophrastus and others but what he produces is not necessarily **anti-feminist literature**. The sources have been changed by being put in the mouth of the Wife of Bath. It is as if Chaucer took lots of old men's coats and cut them up into pieces to make a dress. He stitches all the pieces together like a patchwork with some of them upside down and some back-to-front. In the end, you can still recognise bits of material from the coats but they have been turned into something new.

LA VIEILLE (THE OLD WOMAN)

The anti-feminist tradition also provides us with literary sources for the Wife's character. Old women with voracious sexual appetites waiting to leap on men and make their lives miserable were a familiar part of medieval literature. Chaucer's most likely source, however, is a character in Jean de Meun's *Roman de la Rose*. La Vieille (Old Woman) is a retired prostitute who delivers a monologue which is partly a *confessio* and partly a lecture on how to outwit men. In fact, her entire life has been spent trying to get the better of them. Here are her instructions on how a woman should walk down the street:

> she should raise [her dress] at the sides or in front, as if she wanted a little bit of ventilation or as if she was used to tucking it up so that she could walk more easily. In this way she should be careful to let everyone see the fine shape of her exposed foot. And if she wears a coat she should make sure that it does not cover up her lovely body and hide it from view... Therefore, she should lift up the coat in both hands and spread out her arms, whether on clean streets or muddy ones. She should remember the wheel which the peacock makes with his tail and do the same thing with her coat, so that she shows off her body and the fur linings of her clothes, squirrel or whatever expensive fur she has used, to anyone who might be looking at her.

The Wife of Bath knows a few tricks like these but there is far more to her personality than this. La Vieille is no better than a bitter elderly prostitute who has tried to hurt men but has also been hurt herself in the process. Alison does not set out deliberately to hurt anyone. She is only trying to be happy and seems to think that she makes her husbands happy too, in her own way. Unlike La Vieille, the Wife is a defender of marriage. So long as she sets the rules she is happy always to be a wife. La Vieille has none of the Wife's vitality or optimism. And she certainly has none of the Wife's skills of argument. The Wife likes to be admired but she does not need to rely on the attractions of a bit of squirrel fur to get anyone's attention.

THE WIFE OF BATH'S TALE

The source for the *Wife of Bath's Tale* appears to have been an English folktale, a popular story which probably circulated widely in England before Chaucer. The tale the Wife tells is therefore part folktale and part romance as she sets it in the long ago world of King Arthur and his knights.

In addition to Chaucer's tale, two main versions of the story have come down to us. The first of these is by Chaucer's friend, John Gower, who includes it in his *Confessio Amantis*. In this version, an innocent young knight named Florent kills a man in self defence and is set a task by the dead man's relatives: he must find out what women most desire or die. A loathsome old woman tells him that the answer is 'sovereignty' but he must marry her for this information. They marry secretly by night and then the old woman leads Florent to bed. Disgusted, he lies with his back to her but when he turns round he finds that she is young and beautiful. She tells him that she can be beautiful by day (when his friends will see her) or by night (when she is alone with him). Unable to choose he lets her decide. In doing this he breaks the spell placed upon her by her wicked stepmother. She becomes beautiful all the time and they live happily ever after.

The other version of this story is called *The Wedding of Sir Gawain and Dame Ragnell*. This time the test is set by a man who finds King Arthur hunting in his forest. He gives Arthur a year to find out what it is that women most desire, but Arthur's knight, Sir Gawain, begs to take the challenge for him. Gawain encounters an ugly old woman named Dame Ragnell who will trade the answer for Gawain's hand in marriage. Gawain will happily agree to anything for his king even though this woman is even uglier than she is in the other versions (her snotty nose and tusk-like teeth are only some of her charms). The answer to the riddle is the same as always: women most desire sovereignty over men. And Gawain, who behaves very well under the circumstances, marries the old woman in a lavish ceremony. At night when he goes to kiss his bride he finds that she has become beautiful and is offered the usual choice: beautiful by day or by night. Like Florent, he lets her decide and the wicked stepmother's spell is broken.

Therefore, the basic story of the Loathly Lady (as the old woman is known) and the riddle was already familiar. But Chaucer's version is different in a few important respects. The men in the other stories are innocent and good knights. Chaucer's knight is a rapist. Not only that, he is an unknown rapist. In the other versions we know the names of all the people involved. The old women usually tell the knights in advance that they want marriage. Chaucer's Loathly Lady waits until she has the knight completely in her power and then demands her price. Also, the choice at the end is not so simple in Chaucer. It is not just a matter of beauty by day or by night. Instead the question of female virtue is introduced.

All these changes highlight a very important theme in *The Wife of Bath's Prologue and Tale* – the battle between the sexes. The initial act becomes a rape, the ultimate act of male dominance over women. And the hag's revenge is to exert her dominance over the rapist as he agrees blindly to any condition to save his life.

PART SIX

CRITICAL HISTORY

There are many different critical responses and approaches to *The Wife of Bath's Prologue and Tale*. The Wife has been viewed as, among other things, a monster, a psychotic murderer, an elaborate joke, a sympathetic woman, a champion of women, an enemy of women and not a woman at all. In spite of these varied responses, criticism can be roughly divided into various schools of thought. Many critics do not fit easily into one group or another and many seem to use a variety of arguments, but some basic groups still exist.

HISTORICAL CRITICISM

Critics in this group view Chaucer's *Canterbury Tales* in their fourteenth-century context. They believe that knowledge about the history of the period can throw considerable light on the literature. And so, if we understand what it means to be a woman living in the Middle Ages, for example, we will have a better understanding of *The Wife of Bath's Prologue and Tale*.

At one end of the spectrum this has involved critics looking for a real-life Wife of Bath, searching among the records of medieval Bath for a much married Alison who might have been Chaucer's model (Manly, 1926). At the other end, there are critics who feel that Chaucer was not dealing with real-life individuals at all. The idea here is that he was portraying medieval types or 'estates'. This means that the Wife of Bath should be viewed not as an individual woman but as 'Medieval Woman' and the target for Chaucer's **satire** about women in general (Mann, 1973). Other historical critics go further, and argue that in portraying the Wife of Bath we are not supposed to think of women at all. They see Chaucer's tale as an **allegory** (a symbolic story) about the turbulent historical situation (see Historical Background) in which Richard II is being called upon to rule over his people like a good husband (Wilks, 1962). While other authors see in the

Wife a personification of Rhetoric, the art of persuasion through argument (Alford, 1986–7) or a 'personification of rampant "femininity" or carnality' (Robertson, 1962).

NEW HISTORICISM

The 1980s saw the rise of a slightly different kind of historicism, known as New Historicism. While history is still very important, this form of criticism does not try to place *The Wife of Bath's Prologue and Tale* in any one historical context. History is interwoven with social, economic and political factors. Such critics are not attempting to provide historical background information, they believe that literature belongs in a broad cultural context. They would not approve of the idea that Chaucer is presenting us with an **allegory** of Richard II. Richard II may be part of the story but it is far more complicated. Some critics, for example, see the fourteenth century as a time when social boundaries were breaking down. The Wife of Bath then is a product of this new order, no longer an old 'estate' representative of woman, but a character whose 'self' has to be defined anew at a point in history when this was happening to everyone, including Chaucer (Patterson, 1991).

MARXIST CRITICISM

Marxist critics are closely associated with new historicism but their interest lies primarily in the power relations between various classes. Many such critics see the Wife of Bath as challenging the usual medieval power structure. Medieval women would have found themselves at the bottom of the power hierarchy but some critics see Chaucer as **satirising** the system which would have forced young women to trade sex for economic security with old husbands (Aers, 1980). But the Wife's clever use of power means that she is able to escape male domination (Knight, 1986). The fourteenth century underwent many economic changes as England moved closer towards capitalism. And some critics see this economic change as the key to the character of the Wife who, like a successful capitalist, views every-thing – love, sex, marriage – in terms of business (Delaney, 1975).

Of course, some critics believe that a knowledge of the Middle Ages is completely unnecessary for understanding the Wife of Bath. They feel that all we need to know about the text is the text itself and that we can form an opinion of the Wife of Bath solely by looking closely at the language Chaucer uses. This leads some critics to conclude that the Wife is a wholly sympathetic figure (Donaldson, 1975), or that she is a figure of pathos, even tragedy (Coghill, 1949), or that she is a monster with a redeeming vitality. All of these points of view have their defenders.

PSYCHOANALYTIC HISTORICISM

The many contradictions in *The Wife of Bath's Prologue and Tale* have made it a popular text with psychoanalytic critics. They feel that Chaucer has presented us with a very complex character in the Wife of Bath which can be studied as though she were a 'case' for psychoanalysis. She has accordingly been labelled as an alcoholic 'sociopath' unable to form meaningful relationships with other people (Sands, 1977–8); a nymphomaniac who, in spite of her dominatrix tendencies, 'needs to be mastered in the bedroom' (Burton, 1978–9); and a frigid schizophrenic who probably murdered her fourth husband (Rowland, 1972).

DECONSTRUCTIONIST CRITICISM

The inconsistencies in the text which fuel the psychoanalytical responses are also of great interest to the deconstructionists. They focus on the fact that it is often difficult to pin words down to a specific meaning in Chaucer, and also the fact that it is so difficult to discover what is the 'truth' when the Wife is telling us, for example, that she was always faithful to her husbands but also that she never refused a 'good fellow' her sexual favours. But these critics do not want us to look for 'definite' meanings or the 'truth'. They believe that we cannot decide because for every interpretation there is a counter interpretation present in the text (Leicester, 1990; Knapp, 1987).

This way of viewing *The Canterbury Tales* was first proposed in the early twentieth century (Kittredge, 1915). The idea is that the tale and its teller should always be viewed together, because there is a lot that can be learned about the character from the tale he or she tells. Some critics see strong connections between the Wife of Bath and her tale, seeing her yearning for her lost youth in the transformation of the old hag, or unconsciously revealing her own lack of 'gentillesse' in the old woman's lecture (Lumiansky, 1955). However, other critics believe that the connection between tale and teller is not so illuminating and that Chaucer merely assigned each pilgrim a tale roughly suited to their social class (Benson, 1986).

Critics in this category also look at the wider context of the tale to see if it is a response to any other pilgrim, or part of a larger debate. The idea of a 'marriage group' of tales was popular for some time. According to this school of thought, marriage is a key theme in *The Canterbury Tales* and the Wife's views on marriage are intended to be measured against three of the other tales: the Clerk's tale about a supremely patient and loyal wife; the Merchant's tale about an old man and his faithless young wife; and the Franklin's tale about the problems of fidelity and sovereignty in marriage. But this theory has become less popular in recent years as critics have felt that these four tales are not close enough to one another in the ordering of *The Canterbury Tales* as a whole for this theme to be meaningful, and that marriage is too vague a concept to hold them together anyway.

However, even without the 'marriage' connection, many critics still feel that the relationships between the tales are important (Cooper, 1989). Some believe that the matter can be extended to the much larger question of the relationship between sexuality and authority, and that this is an important theme for Chaucer throughout *The Canterbury Tales* (Kaske, 1973). Others prefer to view *The Wife of Bath's Prologue and Tale* in relation to the tales which share the same fragment of the manuscript. We know that the Wife's tale belongs in sequence with those of the Friar and the Summoner. This makes some critics feel that if Chaucer intended there to be any connection between the tales we will find it here. This view takes the emphasis away from marriage or even love as the dominant theme. Instead, the tales in this fragment are seen as explorations of the problems of experience versus authority (East, 1977). Other critics agree with this grouping but interpret it differently. To some, for example, the Wife and Summoner belong together in opposition to the character of the Friar.

FEMINIST CRITICISM

Many of the dramatic critics were keen to find a feminist viewpoint in *The Wife of Bath's Prologue and Tale* and they have this in common with some feminist critics. These feminist scholars find in the Wife of Bath a character standing up for women and insisting on equality at the very least (Martin, 1990). According to this school of thought, the Wife consciously attacks the world of anti-feminism and exposes it for the unfair system that it is. Alison is viewed as being fully in control of the anti-women literature of the Middle Ages which was designed to describe, criticise and control the behaviour of women. Male writers may have opinions about the opposite sex which aim to dehumanise and keep them in a weak position but the Wife challenges this authority. She judges the judges and will fight her corner on their terms if necessary (Mann, 1991).

Some see the Wife as giving a voice for the first time to the excluded, feminine Other. In her we hear and see all the devaluation and exclusion which medieval women endured but about which male texts are almost always silent. However, the Wife need not be seen as offering a direct challenge to this system. Some critics see her as 'mimicking' the texts of male power not because she wants to defeat this power entirely but because she wants to reform it. She is happy to keep it in place but she wants it to accommodate feminine desire (Dinshaw, 1989).

However, other feminist critics take a different view. They argue that the Wife remains a man's creation. In using the misogynists' materials, the Wife does not undermine them or expose them as ridiculous. Instead she is trapped in a 'prison house' of anti-feminist discourse. She is unable to see that her tactics simply reinforce all the stereotypical medieval ideas about women as cruel, emotional and sexually voracious. Chaucer is, therefore, seen as reinforcing anti-feminist views rather than undermining them (Hansen, 1992).

PART SEVEN

BROADER PERSPECTIVES

FURTHER READING

Further illumination of this list will be found in Critical History.

David Aers, *Chaucer, Langland and the Creative Imagination*, Routledge, 1980
> Prologue and tale as satire of the social and economic situation

John A. Alford, 'The Wife of Bath versus the Clerk of Oxford: What their Rivalry Means', *Chaucer Review* 21, 1986–7, pp.108–32
> Presents the Wife as 'Rhetoric' to the Clerk's 'Logic'

C. David Benson, *Chaucer's Drama of Style: Poetic Variety and Contrast in the Canterbury Tales*, University of North Carolina Press, 1986
> The tales interpreted in relation to their contrasting styles

T.L. Burton, 'The Wife of Bath's Fourth and Fifth Husbands and her Ideal Sixth: The Growth of a Marital Philosophy', *Chaucer Review* 13, 1978–9, pp.34–50
> Interpretation of the Wife through her sexual practices

Nevill Coghill, *The Poet Chaucer*, Oxford University Press, 1949
> The Wife of Bath as tragic figure

Helen Cooper, *The Canterbury Tales*, Oxford University Press, 1989
> Introduction to the tales including sources and context

Sheila Delaney, 'Sexual Economics, Chaucer's Wife of Bath and *The Book of Margery Kempe*', *Minnesota Review* 5, 1975, pp.104–15
> The Wife of Bath in the light of medieval economics

Caroline Dinshaw, *Chaucer's Sexual Poetics*, University of Wisconsin Press, 1989
> The Wife's attempt to have 'feminine desire' accepted without destroying male authority

E.T. Donaldson, *Chaucer's Poetry: An Anthology for the Modern Reader*, 2nd ed. Ronald, NY, 1975
> The Wife of Bath in the light of New Criticism

W.G. East, *The Chaucer Review*, 12, 1977, pp.78–82
> For *The Wife of Bath's Prologue and Tale* as exploration of the problem of experience versus authority

Elaine Tuttle Hansen, ' "Of his love daungerous to me": Liberation, Subversion, and Domestic Violence in *The Wife of Bath's Prologue and Tale*' in Peter G. Beidler, *Geoffrey Chaucer: The Wife of Bath*, Bedford Books, Boston and NY, 1996

Robert E. Kaske, 'Chaucer's Marriage Group' in Jerome Mitchell and William Provost, eds, *Chaucer the Love Poet*, University of Georgia Press, 1973
> Presents the conflict between sexuality and authority as the uniting theme of the tales

George Lyman Kittredge, *Chaucer and his Poetry*, Harvard University Press, 1915
> The Wife of Bath in the light of a 'marriage group'

Peggy A. Knapp, 'Deconstructing the *Canterbury Tales*: Pro' in *Studies in the Age of Chaucer* 2, 1987, pp.73–81
> Deconstructionist interpretation

Stephen Knight, *Geoffrey Chaucer*, Basil Blackwell, 1986
> Marxist interpretation

H. Marshall Leicester Jr, *The Disenchanted Self: Representing the Subject in the Canterbury Tales*, University of California Press, 1990
> Deconstructing the Wife of Bath

R.M. Lumiansky, *Of Sondry Folk: The Dramatic Principle in the Canterbury Tales*, University of Texas Press, 1955
> The intimate connection between tale and teller

John M. Manly, *Some New Light on Chaucer*, Holt, NY, 1926
> For the idea that Chaucer had real life models for the Canterbury pilgrims

Jill Mann, *Chaucer and Medieval Estates Satire: The Literature of Social Class and the General Prologue to the Canterbury Tales*, Cambridge University Press, 1973
> Mann argues that Chaucer's characters should be viewed in terms of their medieval 'estate' or type

– *Geoffrey Chaucer*, Harvester Wheatsheaf, 1991
> Feminist reading of Chaucer

Priscilla Martin, *Chaucer's Women: Nuns, Wives and Amazons*, Macmillan, 1990
> ·Wife of Bath as proto-feminist

Lee Patterson, *Chaucer and the Subject of History*, Routledge, 1991
> A new historicist approach

Derek Pearsall, *The Life of Geoffrey Chaucer*, Blackwell, 1992
> Critical biography of Chaucer

D.W. Robertson, Jr., *A Preface to Chaucer: Studies in Medieval Perspectives*, Princeton University Press, 1962
> The Wife as allegorical representative of the Old Law

Beryl Rowland, 'On the Timely Death of the Wife of Bath's Fourth Husband', *Archiv für das Studium der Neuren Sprachen und Literaturen* 209, 1972, pp.273–82
> The Wife as murderer

Donald B. Sands, 'The Non-Comic, Non-Tragic Wife: Chaucer's Dame Alys as Sociopath', *Chaucer Review* 12, 1978, pp.171–82
> Psychoanalytic view of the Wife of Bath

Michael Wilks, 'Chaucer and the Mystical Marriage in Medieval Political Thought', *Bulletin of the John Rylands Library* 44, 1962, pp.489–530
> *The Wife of Bath's Prologue and Tale* as a political allegory

CHRONOLOGY

World events	Chaucer's life	Literary events

1300 Population of British Isles: *c.* 5 million

1309 Papal See moves to Avignon and comes under French control

1313 Indulgences for public sale by Pope Clement V

1315 Death of Jean de Meun, author of part 2 of *Roman de la Rose*, allegorical poem mocking love, women, the Church and those in authority

1319 Death of Jean de Joinville, French chronicler

1321 Edward II forced to abdicate, imprisoned and probably murdered. Edward III accedes to throne, with wife Philippa

1321 Death of Dante Alighieri, author of *Divine Comedy*

1330 Birth of John Gower, friend of Chaucer and author

1331 Birth of William Langland, author

1337 Birth of Jean Froissart, who will become Clerk of the Chamber to Queen Philippa, and author of *Chronicles*, a brilliant history of 14th-century Europe

1338 Beginning of 100 Years War between France and England

1341 Petrarch crowned as laureate poet at Capitol, Rome

1343? Birth of **Geoffrey Chaucer** in London

1346 French routed at Crécy by Edward III and his son the Black Prince

World events	Chaucer's life	Literary events
1349 Black Death reaches England and kills one third of population		
1351 First Statute of Labourers regulates wages in England		
		1353 In Italy, Giovanni Boccaccio finishes his *Decameron*, a collection of 100 bawdy tales
	1357 Chaucer in service of Countess of Ulster, wife of Prince Lionel, 3rd son of Edward III	
1359 Edward III makes unsuccessful bid for French throne	**1359** Serves in army in France, under Prince Lionel; taken prisoner	
	1360 Edward III pays ransom of £16 for Chaucer's freedom	
1361 Black Death reappears in England		
1362 English becomes official language in Parliament and Law Courts		
		1363 Birth of Christine de Pisan, French author of *La Cité des Dames*, listing all the heroic acts and virtues of women
	1365 Marries Philippa Pan (or Payne) de Roet	
	1366 In Spain on diplomatic mission	
	1367 Granted life pension for his services to king; birth of his son Thomas	
	1368 On Prince Lionel's death, his services transferred to John of Gaunt, Duke of Lancaster	

World events	Chaucer's life	Literary events
	1369 In France with John of Gaunt's expeditionary force; begins *Book of the Duchess* on death of Blanche, John of Gaunt's wife	
	1370-3 Sent on diplomatic missions (11 months in Italy)	**1370** *(c.)* William Langland's *Piers Plowman*
	1374 Appointed Controller of the Customs and Subsidy of Wools, Skins and Leather; receives life pension from John of Gaunt	
		1375 *(c.) Sir Gawain and the Green Knight* written
	1376 Receives payment for some secret, unspecified service	
1377 Edward III dies and is succeeded by Richard II, son of the Black Prince	**1377** Employed on secret missions to Flanders, and sent to France to negotiate for peace with Charles V; employed on further missions in France, Lombardy and Italy	
1378 Beginning of the Great Schism: Urban VI elected Pope in Rome, Clement VII in Avignon		
1380 John Wyclif, who attacked orthodox Church doctrines, condemned as heretic. Wyclif's followers translate Bible into vernacular	**1380** *Parliament of Fowls* written; birth of son Lewis. Cecilia Chaumpayne releases Chaucer from charge of '*de raptu meo*'	
1381 Peasant's Revolt under Wat Tyler quelled by Richard II		

World events	Chaucer's life	Literary events

1382 Appointed, in addition, Controller of the Petty Customs

1385 Allowed privilege of appointing deputy to perform his duties as Controller. Probably writes *Legend of Good Women* and *Troilus and Criseyde*

1385-99 Now living in Greenwich

1386 Richard II deprived of power

1386 Deprived of both official posts. Elected Knight of Shire of Kent

1387 Wife Philippa dies. Begins writing *The Canterbury Tales*

1388 In poverty, Chaucer sells his pensions to raise money

1389 Richard II resumes power

1389 Appointed clerk of king's works at Westminster

1389 John Gower completes first version of *Confessio Amantis*

1391 Writes *Treatise on the Astrolabe* for his son Lewis. Resigns as clerk of king's works and becomes deputy forester of royal forest at North Petherton, Somerset

1396 John of Gaunt marries his mistress, Katherine (de Roet), Chaucer's sister-in-law

1399 Richard II forced to abdicate. Henry IV becomes King of England

1400 Richard II dies in prison. Population of British Isles *c.* 3.5 million

1400 Death of Chaucer

1450 Gutenberg produces first printed book in moveable type

allegory an extended metaphor where the author expects the reader to derive a deeper, perhaps historical or political, meaning in the text

anti-feminist literature medieval literature which criticises women

genre the group or family to which a text belongs, e.g., tragedy, comedy, fairy tale

irony saying one thing but meaning something else

metaphor a comparison in which something is said to 'be' something else

satire literature that exposes wickedness or folly and makes them appear ridiculous

simile a comparison in which something is said to be 'like' something else

AUTHOR OF THIS NOTE

J.A.Tasioulas is a lecturer in English Studies at the University of Stirling. She received an M.A. in English Language and Literature from the University of Glasgow and a D.Phil. in medieval English from the University of Oxford. She was formerly a Junior Fellow at New College, Oxford. She has published on Old and Middle English literature and culture.

NOTES